INTERSECTIONS

The Elements of Fiction
in
Science Fiction

INTERSECTIONS

The Elements of Fiction
in
Science Fiction

Thomas L. Wymer
Alice Calderonello
Lowell P. Leland
Sara Jayne Steen
R. Michael Evers

The Popular Press
Bowling Green State University
Bowling Green, Ohio

ISBN: 0-87972-096-4

Library of Congress catalog card number: 78-61580

Cover design by Don Clausing

CONTENTS

I.   Introduction to Fiction   1

II.   Introduction to Science Fiction   4

III.   Plot   20

IV.   Character   33

V.   Setting   44

VI.   Point of View   56

VII.   Language   67

VIII.   Tone   82

IX.   Theme and Value   89

X.   Symbol and Myth   100

Appendices

A.   A Bibliography of Short Fiction and Poetry
      Cited in the Text   123

      Key to Anthologies and Collections   125

B.   A Critical Bibliography of Science Fiction   128

FOREWORD

Because of the popular appeal of science fiction, most bookstores have numerous shelves reserved for these works; indeed, it is not unusual to find the science fiction section of a bookstore the most crowded browsing area. Though the books that have been and are being turned out vary greatly in quality, there are a large number of serious, gifted writers who have produced works which are coming to be recognized as an important part of our literary tradition. And science fiction is not only worthy of attention as literature; it is also an important part of our culture. According to Robert Scholes and Eric Rabkin, science fiction writers "have been trying to create a modern conscience for the human race."

Whether science fiction is read purely for entertainment or for illumination, its study as literature will surely enhance the reader's appreciation. Thus, this book is designed as a supplementary text for an introduction to literature course built around science fiction. It is divided into chapters that explain and illustrate fundamental literary elements such as plot, characterization, and theme, in terms of both how they function in fiction generally and how they are adapted to science fiction. Although the book contains no history of science fiction, every chapter was written with the concern for making the student aware that there is a literary tradition as well as a tradition of science fiction literature.

Intersections is also designed to be adaptable to any of a variety of available anthologies and selected longer fiction. The examples cited are discussed in such a way viii.

that the student does not need to have read them, although they are many of the most often reprinted works of science fiction. To aid the teacher or student in locating specific cited stories of special interest, a bibliography of such works has been appended, together with location notes to some of the most commonly used or available anthologies. Also appended is a critical bibliography for those who wish to do more reading about science fiction.

This book does not assume any special knowledge of literary forms or structures on the part of the student, nor any acquaintance with science fiction beyond, perhaps, a nodding acquaintance with popular films, television series, and a miscellaneous story or two. Special care was taken to write the book to an audience of General Studies students, many of whom may not read extensively; most of the sections have been class tested with such students, who found the explanations accessible and provocative.

Lastly, the writers wish to add a note of special thanks to Mrs. Marian Burtscher, who, with remarkable patience, energy, and skill, typed not one but two drafts of the entire book.

AN INTRODUCTION TO FICTION

Story telling is one of the oldest and most universal activities of human beings. Stories appeal to people of all ages and levels of sophistication, from the youngest and most naive to the oldest and wisest. The most ancient cultures have left evidence of their stories; isolated, non-technological cultures discovered in modern times have their stories; and modern cultures all have a rich tradition of stories, many of which have become international in popularity.

Why this is so no one fully understands, but there are a number of characteristics of literature and the literary response which suggest reasons. First, we tell stories for entertainment. We seem to enjoy stories in part for their own sake, because we take delight in imagining events we cannot see and in partaking in them through the medium of the story. Perhaps we enjoy the sense of order a story usually implies, with its beginning, middle and end, its quality of formal order which most of our lives do not seem to exhibit. Secondly, we tell stories to inform or instruct. Stories are often created for educational purposes, to portray characters who are models of behavior, both good and evil, or to illustrate facts or morals which the story teller or the culture as a whole believes to be important. Thirdly, we tell stories to illuminate. Stories have been the means of exploring the deepest mysteries of existence, of questioning the basis of our behavior and morals, and of expressing our understanding of our human natures.

These characteristic purposes and effects of literature should not be seen as rigid classifications, since the best literature seems to possess something of all three. A story that merely entertains may give us a sense of momentary pleasure, but our imaginations often demand something more substantial; we need to feel that we are enjoying something "significant" or "meaningful," whatever these words may mean to us. On the other hand, a story that attempts to instruct and does not entertain will probably not instruct very well either. And a story which truly illuminates will entertain us as well, both in that it captures and holds our attention long enough for the illumination to take place and in that the illumination itself is a source of fulfillment and joy.

If these effects of stories are so universal, then one might well ask why we need to take a course in literature. Aren't we already fully capable of enjoying it? The fact is that most readers are not and need at least some help. There are many reasons for this, some of the most important of which follow as a consequence of the nature of the medium of literature, which is language, especially the written language. We can run into various difficulties with language which study and exercise can overcome. We may not listen enough to what we read and therefore fail to respond to effects of sound and rhythm being produced. We may not sufficiently imagine what we read; words, especially as employed by a literary artist, are often indicators of sense experience, of sight, hearing, smell, touch and taste, but too often our reading habits tend to transform words on the page immediately into abstract concepts, and we may miss the significance of an experience that has to be imagined. Literature can deal with an infinite range of experience, and because its medium is language, literature can concern everything that flows from language, which is the repository and transmitter of the vast majority of our history, our knowledge and understanding, our values. And although literature may teach us many things, no single work can teach everything. Each work has to start somewhere, has to assume a certain level of language sophistication in the reader, and sometimes that level is above our own competency. The result may be that we draw a complete blank with the work or that we understand it only on a relatively simple level. In either case our ability to respond to language can be improved and we can understand and enjoy more.

It should be made clear, however, that we are not engaging in some sort of game of looking for "hidden meanings." The fact is that meaning is rarely deliberately concealed in a work of art. If meaning seems hidden this is usually because it is being made manifest in ways to which we have not yet learned to respond. Indeed, some of those ways may seem indirect and lead us to complain, "Why didn't he come right out and say it?" The answer is that in most cases whatever point the artist had to make would most likely have lost its power if he had. Fiction derives its power from its presentation of experience as lived, and its ideas move us deeply because we are led to feel as though we have discovered them in life. A philosopher will ask us what the meaning of death is; a literary artist will present a person dying and shape that presentation so that *we* ask the question. And if he offers an answer, it will tend to be not a set of abstract statements but something lived and felt as well as thought. Not that abstractions are bad: they can help us understand our experience, but they don't mean much until we have discovered some concrete basis for them in our actual or imagined experience. Literature most typically seeks that basis and attempts to set us up for some sort of shock of recognition; that is one of its major gifts to us. Unfortunately, it is not a gift which we can receive passively. It demands effort and skill and knowledge and openness from us.

AN INTRODUCTION TO SCIENCE FICTION

Science fiction can be most broadly defined as a literary response to the rise of modern science. Attempts to define it more specifically have been many, but our concern here is not so much to decide on some narrower definition as to learn something of its various types and possible forms so that we will be more able to enjoy it. How then has literature responded to modern science?

Rather than answer this question with a straight historical account of the development of science fiction over the last two centuries, it would suit our purposes better if we considered what science fiction does in terms of the same broad categories we used to describe the general purposes of fiction: to entertain, to inform and to illuminate. As before, we will discuss each as a sort of pure end, remembering that most science fiction will manifest more than one of these ends.

Science Fiction as Entertainment

As a form of entertainment, science fiction reveals a genealogy which goes back to some of the most ancient literary traditions. Thomas D. Clareson, a major critic and historian of science fiction, likes to point out that much of science fiction can be directly related to the heroic or epic mode of Homer, eighth century B.C. author of *The Iliad* and *The Odyssey,* of the anonymous seventh century A.D. author of *Beowulf,* and of Sir Thomas Malory, fifteenth century author of *Le Morte d'Arthur* (see the introduction to *Many Futures, Many Worlds,* ed. Clareson, listed in Critical Bibliography). In the heroic and epic modes, the primary narrative pattern is a quest of some sort, and emphasis is on action and adventure. Another similar tradition is that of the fantastic voyage, which again emphasizes action and adventure but with even greater emphasis on the wonder to be found in remote corners of the earth. Homer's *Odyssey* is also an example of this type, as are numerous fantastic medieval travel books.

Such works are not, of course, science fiction, but they provided the basic narrative patterns which were adapted to new possibilities opened up by modern science. We can see something of how this was done by glancing at a few of the sciences, starting with geography. Throughout the nineteenth and into the twentieth century there remained large regions of the world unexplored by Western peoples: darkest Africa, large portions of South and Central America, both poles. What might be there? Science fictional explorations inevitably preceded the actual explorers, and produced classics such as H. Rider Haggard's *She* (1887), the story of a man's discovery in Africa of the lost valley of Kor, ruled by a voluptuous and immortal pagan princess, and Arthur Conan Doyle's *The Lost World* (1912), which recounts an expedition to the headwaters of the Amazon, where a lost plateau confines and conceals wonders of a different sort.

Explorations such as these were not based only on gaps in geographical knowledge, however. The fiction writers' dreams were inspired by the findings of other sciences. Archeology produced a succession of wonderful finds during the second half of the nineteenth century, including biblical cities like Babylon and Nineveh and most especially a series of lost cities thought to be only mythical, Troy, Mycenae, Knossus, and many more. The intriguing idea that similar cities and civilizations might still exist in some far corner of the earth, not buried by the sands of time but only separated from us by their remoteness, inspired such fictional creations as the Valley of Kor, the central African domain of Haggard's Ayesha, She-Who-Must-Be-Obeyed.

Paleontology revealed the fossil remains of real "dragons" like Tyrannosaurus Rex and Allosaurus, creatures like the Pterodactyl that only nightmare, it would seem, could spawn, but which actually roamed the sky millions of years ago. Might these monsters still survive in some other corner of the earth? Indeed, many scientists of the nineteenth century thought so, since they were reluctant to believe that God or nature would produce a species, let it thrive for millions of years, and then let it disappear into extinction. Conan Doyle used such speculations as the basis for Professor Challenger's discovery and exploration of a plateau deep in the Amazon jungle inhabited by dinosaurs.

During much of the nineteenth century geologists entertained the theory that the earth might be hollow, with openings at one or both of the poles, a theory exploited by numerous writers from Edgar Allan Poe in *The Narrative of A. Gordon Pym* (1838) to Jules Verne in *A Journey to the Center Of the Earth* (1864). By 1914, however, when *At The Earth's Core,* the first of Edgar Rice Burroughs' Pellucidar series, was published in *All Story Magazine,* the hollow earth had been relegated to the realm of science fantasy.

And of course new technological inventions and discoveries made it possible for stories to concentrate as much or more on the means of travel as on the places seen. Such stories, made famous by Jules Verne in works like *Five Weeks in a Balloon* (1863) and *Twenty Thousand Leagues under the Sea* (1870), came to form a special subdivision of science fiction adventure called gadget fiction.

In short, then, science fiction offered the opportunity for extending into the modern world the heroic actions and imaginary voyages of the ancient past in a context that could seem more plausible than myth, fairy tale or fantasy. And that context continued to develop as science developed: as the lost race story was the major form of science fiction action-adventure from around 1880 to around 1920, for the next quarter century space opera took over with many of the same kinds of stories expanded first to an interplanetary, then to a galactic scale. A parallel development was a shift from an interest in sciences like geology and archeology to ones like astronomy and physics.

The more purely entertaining forms of science fiction, however, are not limited to traditional action-adventure. Science fiction has also adapted other forms like the Gothic and detective stories and created a form of its own, the puzzle story.

Gothic stories, called so because of their early identification with stories in medieval settings, are more descriptively called tales of terror. For some reason most human beings seem to derive pleasure out of being frightened—in contexts where they can't really be hurt. That fact has supported a considerable production of terror fiction, especially since the late eighteenth century, and a much more lucrative production of terror films in more recent years. Mary Shelley in *Frankenstein* (1818) was the first to combine the tale of terror with the possibilities of natural science to produce not only the first story of a scientifically created monster but the first science fiction horror story. The combination of science and terror has been used as well by such writers as Edgar Allan Poe, H.P. Lovecraft and Ray Bradbury and is still very much alive, most typically for science fiction in stories of alien encounters. A good example of the connection is "Who Goes There?" (1938), a novellette by John W. Campbell, Jr. An Antarctic expedition discovers the frozen body of an extraterrestrial creature which they dig free and thaw out, a situation which recalls the horror story motif of digging up a monster from a grave. The alien monster, once un-iced, revives and turns out to be a shape changer, going the vampire one better by being able to absorb any creature and become a perfect imitation of it, which again recalls a horror story motif, demonic possession. The expedition members realize that any one or more of their number could be monsters, and they set about trying to discover and destroy the demons among them.

The detective story is another form freely adapted by science fiction. In its classic form the detective story centers on some sort of crime and one or more of several questions, such as who committed the crime or how the crime was committed or how can the criminal be proved guilty (all are such common story lines that they each have names: the whodunit, the howdunit, and the howzegonnacatchim). The science fiction detective story usually plays the game of answering the crucial questions about a crime in a society in which the rules have been altered because the crime takes place in the future. In Alfred Bester's *The Demolished Man* (1951), for instance, crime is almost non-existent because the police are telepaths. But, since most people are not telepaths, there are something like constitutional safeguards which require the police to convict criminals by kinds of evidence close to today's conventions. These conditions create a special challenge for a ruthless and intelligent man to commit the perfect crime. From the point of view of the detective, whodunit is easily solved, while howzegonnacatchim becomes the major problem. But Bester also throws in a crucial element of whydunit that complicates the question of motive, and adds a taste of the psychological thriller: the murderer does not himself know the deepest reasons for his having committed the crime.

Although *The Demolished Man* is one of the best known of science fiction detective stories, the most famous practitioner is Isaac Asimov, who has written two science fiction detective novels, *Caves of Steel* (1954) and *The Naked Sun* (1956), and a number of short stories, including four featuring armchair detective Dr. Wendell Urth.

The puzzle story is more exclusively the domain of science fiction. Although no crime is involved, it is like the

classic detective story in that it presents an intellectual
problem or puzzle and challenges the reader to figure out
the answer before it is revealed in the story. Also like the
detective, it is most effective if most readers cannot
anticipate the answer yet feel they should have known it.
Murray Leinster's "First Contact," a classic example of
the type, concerns an encounter between space ships from
Earth and an alien planet millions of miles from either
home planet. Both seem willing to establish peaceful
relations, but each is afraid that the other might be hostile
and might be able to trail the other back home, using that
knowledge to launch a surprise attack without fear of
retaliation (published in 1945, the story betrays a fresh
memory of Pearl Harbor). At first it appears that the only
answer is for each to attack the other: if both or even if
only one is destroyed, both home planets will remain
unknown to the other and therefore safe. Humans and
aliens seem unwilling to accept so drastic a solution,
however; but unless someone comes up with a better
idea.... Can parting as friends be arranged so that it is
impossible for either to discover the source of the other?

Asimov is also one of the most accomplished
practitioners of the puzzle story, most notably in his robot
stories. For that series he created The Three Laws of
Robotics, with the help of John W. Campbell, Jr., not only
a writer but the most famous editor of the period 1938-
1950:

1. A robot may not injure a human being, or through
inaction allow a human being to come to harm.

2. A robot must obey the orders given it by human
beings except where such orders would conflict with the
First Law.

3. A robot must protect its own existence as long as
such protection does not conflict with the First or Second
Law.

These laws constitute a very neat, logical structure, a set
of rational givens or axioms which always remain true
and which Asimov applies to particular situations: robots

are behaving in unusual ways; what is wrong, how can the situation be set right? Typically the answer is to be found in some new understanding of what the laws really say, some manipulation of the situation in order to make the laws work as desired, or some new application of the laws.

In "Runaround," one of the stories from Asimov's collection, *I, Robot,* Gregory Powell and Mike Donovan are managing a mining operation on Mercury with the help of a robot named Speedy. They have sent Speedy out on the sunside of Mercury, a region too hot for humans in their best protective suits to survive more than a few minutes, in order to acquire some selenium, a substance necessary for the repair of their damaged solar power equipment. But the robot is running in circles around the selenium pool, out of range of radio contact. What's wrong with the robot and how can they get him back before the mining station runs out of power in a few hours? As Powell analyzes the problem, Speedy was simply ordered to get the selenium and not told that the humans were in danger; therefore, Rule One is not operating. In trying to get the selenium, Speedy is following orders, or Rule Two. But because he is an especially advanced and expensive model, Rule Three has been strengthened in Speedy; approaching the molten selenium is dangerous even for a robot; therefore Speedy is trapped in a kind of equilibrium between the demands of Rules Two and Three. What can be done? After an interesting answer is tried out and proved ineffective, Powell comes up with the only solution: to walk out toward Speedy beyond the point where the man's "insosuit" protects him; Speedy will see the man in immediate danger of death, and Rule One, not allowing a human to come to harm through inaction, should override Speedy's run-around between Two and Three—Powell hopes. He is correct. Most of these stories are somewhat like those puzzles one finds in logic text books, presented in a more elaborate fictional context. The result is the more intellectual form of entertainment associated with problem-solving games.

Notice that science fiction as entertainment embraces
both the analytic joys of abstract problem solving
associated with "hard" science fiction, called so because
of its emphasis on scientific detail and accuracy, and the
emotional and physical satisfactions of action-adventure
associated with "soft" science fiction, called so because of
its carelessness about or at least lack of emphasis on
accurate or plausible scientific fact. Indeed, some of the
best science fiction combines both joys, since certain
kinds of action and adventure can be found in the
scientific quest for knowledge, in research and
development, in trial, error and discovery. Many
scientists today will confess that their being professional
scientists owes much to their having been first attracted
to the drama, excitement and adventure of scientific
investigation and discovery by science fiction.

Science Fiction as Instruction

Instruction of one kind or another has long been a
major concern of science fiction, more so than most forms
of fiction. Among the reasons for this are two of special
importance.

The first concerns a kind of instruction science fiction
is forced to give. Anyone who feels intimidated by all the
science in science fiction will be comforted to know that
most authors cannot and do not assume that their
audience understands all the scientific facts or laws that
may be necessary to the working out of their plots. If it is
necessary for us to know the Second Law of
Thermodynamics or to understand the concept of inertia
or to picture a moebius strip, usually the author will
somehow provide the necessary explanations within the
story—and usually in a much more effective way than we
are likely to find in a text book. In other words, a
substantial amount of scientific knowledge is not a
prerequisite to understanding science fiction. The reverse

is more likely, that in reading science fiction with attention we will probably learn a good deal about science and will find ourselves stimulated to want to learn more. This is true even in a puzzle story where, if our curiosity is effectively aroused, we will enjoy discovering an answer we could not have figured out for ourselves. We enjoy the learning experience, the satisfaction of grasping, especially in a context which has engaged our imagination so much that the answer seems to really matter to us.

The second reason for the concern for instruction in science fiction involves its more direct interest in informing the reader. Fiction is an effective way to gain a reader's attention in order to communicate complex information to him or her. We can see this fact in operation in what might be called the pre-science fiction form of the utopia. It began with Plato as a theoretical discussion of the structure of an ideal society. By the sixteenth century, however, Thomas More combined an interest in hypothetical social structures with the imaginary voyage and presented his *Utopia* (1516) as the personal account of a voyage to a distant land by a fictional character, Raphael Hythloday. Thereafter, the imaginary voyage became a common fictional framework for political and social treatises and satires of all sorts.

As early as the seventeenth century similar adaptations were being made from the scientific treatise. In a work most commonly translated as *Kepler's Dream* (1634), Johannes Kepler, an early seventeenth century German astronomer (he corrected Copernicus by showing that the planetary orbits around the Sun were elliptical, not circular), presented what amounted to a treatise on lunar astronomy in the literary form of the medieval dream vision: a moon demon appears in a dream to the central character and explains to him the nature of the moon. In addition to using fiction as a means of entertaining readers and retaining their interest, Kepler may well have been deliberately disguising the scientific content of his work. In a time in which thinkers were being persecuted for publishing observations or speculations at odds with accepted religious dogma, Kepler may have used fiction both to protect himself and to infiltrate scientific ideas into otherwise unreceptive minds.

This is an extreme case, more treatise than fiction, but even in works where more attention is paid to fiction, instruction can still be of major importance. This is evident in a story like H.G. Wells' "The Star," in which the earth suffers a near miss by a quasi-stellar body that comes into our solar system from interstellar space. Wells uses the story to impress upon his late nineteenth century audience the immensity of the cosmos, the precariousness of human existence, subject as it is to natural laws operating in an indifferent universe, and the importance to human dignity of understanding those laws as opposed to being their ignorant victim.

Wells feels the need to impress this knowledge on his audience because of a problem which has existed since the beginning of modern science, the ignorance and prejudice displayed toward science by large portions of both the general public and those who see themselves as spokesmen for religious or human values. This is a problem that was faced by men like Copernicus and Galileo in the sixteenth and seventeenth centuries, by Charles Darwin and Thomas Henry Huxley (one of Wells' professors) in the nineteenth, and it is a problem still very much with us. In "The Two Cultures," an important and controversial essay published in 1956, C.P. Snow argued:

the intellectual life of the whole of western society is increasingly being split into two polar groups...: at one pole we have the literary intellectuals, who incidentally while no one was looking took to referring to themselves as "intellectuals" as though there were no others..., at the other scientists, and as the most representative, the physical scientists. Between the two a gulf of mutual incomprehension—sometimes (particularly among the young) hostility and dislike, but most of all lack of understanding. ("The Two Cultures," *New Statesman,* 6 October 1956; reprinted in Snow, *The Two Cultures and a Second Look,* Cambridge: Cambridge University Press, 1959).

The attempt to bridge this gap by promoting scientific and technological literacy through fiction is one of the most distinguishing characteristics of science fiction.

It would be a mistake, however, to suggest that science fiction is consistent in its attitude toward this issue. Within the genre we will find everything from blanket condemnation of all science and technology as evil to the belief that scientific breakthroughs will bail us out of all our problems and set the world straight, what sometimes amounts to a worship of science as almost a new religion. Mary Shelley comes close to the first extreme when she presents the awakening of the passion for knowledge in Dr. Frankenstein as a kind of fall from grace into evil; good examples of the second extreme are A.E. van Vogt's "The Weapon Shop" (1942) and *The World of Null A* (1945). Whatever its position, however, the most intellectually responsible science fiction tries to base whatever position it takes on solid information and reasonable speculation rather than attacking or promoting science and technology as some kind of black or white magic. And in order to communicate its position, it usually engages in some sort of instruction.

Incidentally, science fiction suffers its own "two cultures" problem. The science fiction of the 1940s and 1950s was dominated by a pro-science bias and a rather limited awareness of the wider literary culture. Isaac Asimov's claim that science fiction is "the *only* literature of relevant ideas, since it is the only literature that, at its best, is firmly based on scientific thought," is typical of this attitude (Asimov, "When Aristotle Fails, Try Science Fiction," *Intellectual Digest,* 2 [December 1971], 75). The 1960s saw the emergence of a more literarily selfconscious

group of writers, such as Norman Spinrad, Thomas
Disch, Ursula K. Le Guin, J.G. Ballard, Harlan Ellison
and many others, who came to be called the "new wave."
Both groups, however, were still trying to bridge the same
gap, differing primarily in emphasis: members of the first
group thought of themselves as scientifically literate
people who wrote stories, while those of the second saw
themselves as literary people who were scientifically
aware.

Science Fiction as Illumination

We have already drifted into the topic of illumination
in the previous section, especially in the discussion of
Wells. This happened simply because instruction is rarely
the chief purpose of science fiction; it usually occurs as an
element secondary to entertainment or illumination. But
the difference between instruction and illumination needs
clarification.

Whereas instruction involves the transmission of
specific information, illumination involves the
integration of new knowledge into our sense of value.
Wells instructs us by explaining something of the relative
sizes and distances involved in the solar system, by
revealing that the motions of bodies through it can be
predicted with a fair degree of accuracy, and by implying
that the overwhelming majority of human beings in his
time, the supposedly civilized as well as the primitive
savage, are utterly ignorant of these facts. He attempts to
illuminate by suggesting that the knowledge of these
facts is important to our humanity. It is a knowledge
made to strike us as both humbling and exalting,
humbling in its revelation of our smallness before the
immensity of time and space and exalting in its
implication that through knowledge of that immensity we
partake of it and even rise above it.

We can see something of the ways in which science
fiction illuminates by considering some of the variations

that can occur in the types of entertainment science fiction we have noted. The best heroic action-adventure, including the work of Homer, critically examines the nature of heroism itself. Frank Herbert does this in *Dune* (1965), a story clearly cast in the action-adventure mold, with epic battles and a final triumph. But it is also a story in which the hero discovers that the more he seems to control events, the more they come to control him; he also finds that his greatest triumph leads to a galactic war, a state of affairs he most wanted to avoid. Heroic fantasies appeal in part to our desire to be good, to serve mankind, but they also appeal to our sense of insecurity, to our desire for power and mastery, to our need to imagine ourselves in control. To discover that such desires can lead a good or even great person as easily to tyranny as to heroism is to discover something important about our humanity.

Tales of terror may illuminate by exploring and critically examining our fears. We can see the difference between terror tales that illuminate and those that do not by looking at some typical alien encounter stories. In the rather unilluminating pulp science fiction of the 1930s the most common sort of alien was the BEM, the Bug-Eyed Monster, an unambiguously evil creature whom the hero had to figure out how to destroy and whom we could feel unselfconsciously satisfied in seeing destroyed. But the best monsters owe their effectiveness to the ways in which they remind us, either consciously or unconsciously, of real things we fear. A good example from a comparatively late BEM story is the alien creature in "Arena," by Fredric Brown. Carson, the human hero of the story, calls it a "Roller" because it looks like a red ball, a "red sphere of terror," which propels itself along the ground by rolling. It is described as "utterly alien, horribly different," so different that Carson is forced to conclude, "the universe was not a place that could hold" both Man and Roller: "Further apart than god and devil, there could never be even a balance between them." This attitude reflected the times, for the story was first published in 1944, when the red circle on the Japanese flag represented to Americans an object of fear and loathing equal to Carson's red sphere.

This kind of historical connection may be illuminating in itself, but the story does not call attention to the connection or explore the validity of the fear. Brown simply exploits the ready-made symbol which evokes fear.

By contrast, the alien encounter story of the 1960s and 1970s is more likely to reveal overt connections between our fears and our racial and cultural prejudices. We may well find that the alien at first thought to be monstrous is really much like us, or even morally superior, reminding us of peaceful Amerindians or Vietnamese farmers, while the white human turns out to be the real monster, unable or unwilling to understand the alien creatures because he is too concerned with stealing their land or other resources or otherwise exploiting or "saving" them, or simply because he is too wrapped up in his own cultural assumptions and prejudices to recognize that other cultures might wish to be different from him.

The detective story has long offered an effective means of exploring the various levels of contemporary society, as we follow the detective through the streets of the modern city, seeking out the criminal. To a science fiction author like Isaac Asimov who wants to describe a future or alternative world, the detective's quest in a novel like *Caves of Steel* offers a much more interesting reason for exploring the city than the kind of guided tour we so often find in utopias. Moreover, the detective story offers interesting opportunities for other kinds of speculation. Imagine a future technological utopia in which all man's basic needs are satisfied. Would there still be crime? If, as many people think, the social structure somehow contributes to the creation of criminals, would future changes in the social system create changes in criminal patterns? Will laws, the definitions of crime, change substantially in the future? What might the impact of new technologies, like vast computerized information systems or listening devices from micro-miniaturized "bugs" to long-range microwave microphones, be upon techniques of crime detection and on protections of our privacy?

The puzzle story offers interesting possibilities for explorations of what really constitutes an answer or solution to human problems. Tom Godwin's "The Cold Equations" makes a point about the limitations of man's manipulations of natural law. We are presented with what looks like a classic puzzle situation in which it seems impossible to save the life of a young girl who has stowed away on a small space ship, impossible because there is not enough fuel to land both her and the pilot. Suspense is maintained to a large degree through the expectation, created by the puzzle tradition itself, that someone will come up with an ingenious solution at the last minute. No one does. To some problems there are no happy solutions.

The opportunities for illumination, for expanding our awareness and understanding of ourselves and our universe, are truly infinite—in both science fiction and in fiction in general. But science fiction is an especially fertile form because of the opportunities it offers for testing our assumptions, prejudices and values through exaggerated or extreme situations or radically altered conditions which throw into sharp relief our preconceptions. The result is what one critic, Darko Suvin, calls *cognitive estrangement*. ("On the Poetics of the Science Fiction Genre," *College English* 34[December 1972], 372-83; reprinted in Rose, in Critical Bibliography). That is, we are led to look upon the norms of any age as though they were unfamiliar, unique, changeable. We are on the outside looking in upon every imaginable world, *including our own,* as a theoretical model. This sense of estrangement is cognitive in that it encourages us to question and analyze the norms and values operating in the world or society under observation. Certainly the more science fiction tends toward pure entertainment, the less cognitive it is and the more we are led simply to enjoy the sense of strangeness, but the general result of reading a cross-section of science fiction should be an expanded awareness of ourselves and of all our possible contexts.

PLOT

Plot is the series of related incidents or events within a story. We are usually talking about plot when we summarize the action of the story,although, as anyone who has tried it well knows, summary itself can be a complex process. Characters' thoughts, for instance, are as much actions as are their movements in space, and motivations, both internal and external, clarify the causes and significance of action. Plot, in other words, includes not only what happens but why.

Although the variety of possible plots is infinite, there are certain elements that seem to be repeated in most stories and which form the basis for a kind of standard plot and some of the many variations and departures from it.

Perhaps the most universal element of plot is *conflict*, the opposition between characters or forces, the working out of which makes up the story. Conflicts can be external or internal. External conflicts include *human against human,* in which individuals or groups oppose each other, or *human against the environment,* whether natural or social. In internal conflicts, *human against self,* individuals are pitted against some aspect of their own minds.

For science fiction, however, we have to modify these clarifications slightly. Human against human has to become *sentient creature against sentient creature,* since one or both of the conflicting individuals or groups may be nonhuman, intelligent creatures. Another modification is necessitated by the fact that science fiction so often uses the situations it creates as a basis for debate. More commonly than in other types of fiction we are likely to find that conflicts between individuals or groups are also conflicts between ideas or ideologies. In Isaac Asimov's "Nightfall," for instance, the major conflict is between scientists and fanatic believers in a religious faith called the Cult. More broadly, however, the conflict as Asimov sets it up is between people who believe in the scientific method as a means of gaining truer understanding of the universe and people who believe in an ancient document as the literal source of eternal and unchanging truth. In short, it is a rather extreme case of a conflict between Science and Religion.

Conflicts of human against the environment also take on special dimensions in science fiction. Again, the first term in the conflict should be changed from human to sentient creature. The nature with which the sentient creature is in conflict is most likely an alien environment of some sort, outer space or some planet other than Earth which offers special problems of survival: extremes of heat or cold like Mercury or Pluto, extremes of gravity like Jupiter, extremely thin or poisonous or high-pressure atmospheres like Mars, Venus, or Jupiter, or unusual or dangerous plant or animal life. And, of course, seen from the point of view of an extraterrestrial, Earth could be a hostile, alien environment. Most typically the struggle is for survival by means of either conquest and control of, or understanding and adaptation to, the environment. Extreme forms of conflict with the natural environment have been built around such concepts as "terraforming" (the alteration of a planet's life-supporting properties to conform to those of Earth) and biological adaptation (the alteration of the human form to make possible its survival in an alien environment). Walter M. Miller, Jr.'s "Crucifixus Etiam," which concerns a project on Mars for increasing the atmosphere by freeing oxygen from trapped underground ice, is an example of the former; Clifford Simak's "Desertion," built around a machine which transforms humans into the physical form of animals native to Jupiter, exemplifies the latter.

Conflicts of sentient creatures with the social environment take on many forms. In "The Machine Stops," E.M. Forster portrays a world of human beings who have surrendered control of their lives to a machine that provides everything for their comfort. The central character comes in conflict with his world when he begins to wonder whether humanity is being helped or crippled by the Machine. In "The Subliminal Man," J.G. Ballard imagines a world dominated by an economic system demanding constant growth in production and sales. To promote those sales a vast system of subliminal advertising is being installed to stimulate people unconsciously to buy products they don't need; this system has begun to turn the whole populace into mindless consumers. Conflicts with the social environment in science fiction tend to reflect the modern awareness of how we can be victimized not so much by individuals as by whole economic, technological, or political systems.

Internal conflicts, *the individual against himself,* are centered in the mind of a character. Robert Silverberg's "Sundance" concerns a kind of terraforming, in this case the extermination of a planet's major species of animal life, "Eaters," which are seen from the human point of view as "ecology wreckers,...devourers of oxygen-liberating plants." But the Eaters, "spherical, bulky, slow-moving creatures covered by masses of coarse orange fur," offer no resistance, and no major conflict exists with the external environment. Rather the chief conflict is in the mind of a human, Tom Two Ribbons, who still recalls his Amerindian ancestry and is torn with guilt over what could be terrible waste, or worse, murder: sometimes he sees the creatures his team is killing as something like American bison; sometimes he suspects that they are sentient and imagines them to be like his own ancesters, similarly exterminated by a technologically superior culture. The plot, therefore, centers on Tom's internal struggle to come to terms with himself, with his past, with his confused perceptions, and with the actions of himself and his companions.

A work of fiction usually develops any one or more of the above types of conflict within a structural framework. The structure may closely follow a logical development in a standard or classic pattern, or it may be developed by variations of this pattern. The classic pattern, which can be seen in Miller's "Crucifixus Etiam," usually begins with the *exposition,* the revelation of character, setting and conflict. In the Miller story we are told in the first few paragraphs that Manue Nanti is the main character, that he is on Mars in 2134 A.D. as a laborer in a project of which he knows very little, and that he is painfully struggling in Mars' thin atmosphere not to surrender the maintenance of his life processes entirely to his mechanical aerator, a device which does the work of lungs, but the use of which gradually destroys the lungs, creating permanent dependence on the machine.

After the exposition, the plot unfolds through a pattern of *rising action.* The conflict deepens and the tension in the story increases. Part of the way this is achieved is through the addition of *complication,* new conflicts that either delay the resolution of the main conflict or come to be revealed as more important conflicts. To Manue's external conflicts with an alien atmosphere and a mechanical device is added a growing sense of conflict with an economic and political system that seems to be exploiting his labor and his lungs. To the internal struggle involved in the temptation to stop breathing and let his lungs atrophy is added the realization that his original goal, to work for five years and return home a wealthy man, does not seem to justify the pain he suffers. And as he loses ground in the struggle to keep his lungs working, he develops a growing need for a purpose high enough to justify his loss. One of the major results of complication and its delaying effect is the addition of *suspense,* the state of anxiety and anticipation

in the reader that results either from uncertainty as to what is to come, how and whether the conflicts will be resolved, or from uncertainty about when something we know is inevitable will happen.

The culmination of the rising action is the *climax*, the physical and emotional high point in the story. In the Miller story, as in many others, that "point" is not a single moment but a closely related series of events involving a pattern of recognition and reversal. *Recognition* is the point where the character gains new insight or knowledge which may lead to a change in his course of movement, or a *reversal*. In this story months have passed and Manue has given up the battle with his aerator—and given up hope as well. But a stage of the job his crew has been working on is completed and a special gathering is called in which the workers are told what they have not known until then, that the project they have been working on is intended to give Mars a breathable atmosphere—a project that will be completed in eight hundred years. This announcement precipitates the beginning of a rebellion, which is stopped when Manue strikes down the rebel leader. Manue's act is certainly the physical high point in the story, and some readers might wish to call it the climax, but it falls short of being the major climax because Manue does not yet understand what he has done. In a period of agonized contemplation described as "Manue's desperate Gethsemane," in which his suffering is compared to that of Christ in the garden before his arrest and crucifixion, Manue undergoes a recognition experience in which he realizes that he would rather be a sower than a reaper. This recognition brings about a reversal, a change in Manue's attitude, a new birth of pride in what he is contributing to, "an eight-century passion of human faith in the destiny of the race of Man.

Finally, the recognition and reversal usually leads to a *resolution,* a final outcome that typically means the relaxation of conflicts. In accepting the aerator and the loss of lung function, Manue is no longer in conflict with the natural environment; in accepting the purpose of the project, he ceases to oppose the economic and political system, of which he is now a willing part rather than an exploited victim; and in that acceptance he discovers a sense of higher purpose which resolves his inner conflicts. It is not at all unusual for a climax to gain power by setting up a simultaneous resolution of more than one conflict.

As can be seen in this discussion, there may be difficulty in locating *the* climax in some stories. It is easy when recognition and reversal take place in the midst of a high point in external action. In other cases it may be debatable, depending on what one sees as the major conflict and, therefore, the highest point of tension. "Crucifixus Etiam" is also somewhat atypical in that there is so little separation between the climax and the resolution. Since the major conflicts are internal, Manue's recognition and reversal resolve those conflicts and the story is over. In other stories a recognition and reversal may still demand some action on the character's part to set things right, to ease remaining tensions, in which case the resolution will be distinct from the climax.

Whatever the case, the sense of a standard plot provides a set of terms and a sense of a framework with which we can discover how a given plot is structured. We can see this by looking at some of the most common varieties of the classic plot structure.

An author may begin a story with action, plunging us immediately into a crisis and letting exposition catch up with us later. For example, this is how Robert Sheckley begins "Specialist":

The photon storm struck without warning, pouncing upon the Ship from behind a bank of giant red stars. Eye barely had time to flash a last second warning through Talker before it was upon them.

Clearly, the reader is catapulted into the middle of

suspenseful action without any sort of preamble or exposure to background information.

Another common variation on the classic plot structure is the mixture of dramatic action with exposition. Asimov begins "Nightfall" with an interview of a scientist by a journalist who, like us, needs to have the background explained to him. Through dialogue the reader is involved in an initial conflict between the two speakers and at the same time given background information and introduced to the major conflicts of the story.

There may be variations in the way climax is handled: there could be more than one climax, for instance. In Asimov's detective novel, *Caves of Steel,* action rises twice to what turn out to be false solutions before we are presented with the real one in the major climax. Sometimes one conflict may be resolved in a minor climax, only to set up a more important conflict for a later climax.

There are also possible variations in the ways recognition and reversal are handled. A character may never achieve recognition or may ironically experience a false recognition, while the reader is set up to discover what the character misses (see also the discussion of irony in the chapter on Tone). In Gene Wolfe's "Eyebem" the central character is a robot that believes itself to be superior to human beings. It maintains that belief to the end of the story, when we see it stranded in an Arctic wilderness, all its memory tapes about to erase automatically as its power pack runs dry (the robot equivalent of death), while its human companion is surviving very well. In effect, the robot undergoes a reversal, but without recognition.

In Ballard's "The Subliminal Man" the reverse happens: the major character undergoes recognition without reversal. The system of subliminal advertising is being constructed without public knowledge. The central character refuses to believe that the government could be doing this to him until the installation is completed. In his last flicker of selfconsciousness he is finally convinced,but that awareness begins to fade as he falls into a pattern of mindless response and becomes a perfect consumer. Recognition is achieved, but it does not bring about a change in the character's course of movement— there is no reversal.

The lack of the central character's recognition in "Eyebem" reveals another common variation, the fact that the major recognition experience can be set up to occur in the reader rather than in any character. A further variation on this pattern occurs in James Blish's "Common Time," where major recognition experiences for character and reader take place at widely separated points in the story. The major recognition for the main character occurs in the middle of the story, rather than more customarily at the end, when Garrard, an astronaut journeying to Alpha Centauri, discovers a race of creatures who are almost like angels in their capacity for love and communion with one another as well as with Garrard. When he returns to Earth, however, Garrard finds the experience fading from his memory; he yearns to return but is forbidden to do so by his own frightened and suspicious superiors. At this point, although Garrard is losing the understanding he achieved earlier, the reader is led to see Garrard's position on Earth as typical of the personal isolation that is humanity's lot. The reader sees more clearly than Garrard that where we are is a kind of hell—or at least a place heartbreakingly far removed from heaven.

"Common Time" also reveals another variation, a *circular* plot structure. The standard plot, which we have seen in "Crucifixus Etiam" and the other stories discussed so far, is by contrast described as *linear* because it moves in a straight line from an initial situation to one of major change, either in characters, external conditions, or both. A circular plot takes us through a pattern of change, but returns us to a state of affairs in some important way much like that in which we started. "Common Time" begins with Garrard in a tense moment, alone on his spaceship shortly after leaving Earth. The middle of the story is characterized by resolution, the release of tension in Garrard's discovery of peace and understanding. The end returns us to a state of tension similar to that at the beginning. Though circular in pattern, however, taking us from tension and isolation to tension and isolation, the plot nevertheless guides us to something new, a new understanding of how we are all alone.

Plots can also be *simple* or *complex,* concentrating, as most stories do, on a single plot line, or weaving together two or more separate plot lines. An example of this kind of plot is Gene Wolfe's "The Island of Dr. Death and Other Stories." The major plot line centers on the attempts of ten-year-old Tackman Babcock to understand who he is as he suffers the neglect of his alcoholic, divorced mother and the indifference of her lover. Mixed in with this plot line is a separate plot which involves Tackman's fantasies inspired by an action-adventure novel he is reading, a story which, with its active, decisive characters, its clear sense of good and evil and heroic purpose, stands in marked contrast to Tackman's "real" world.

Finally, the plot can center on a single unifying action, as Frederik Pohl's "Day Million" centers on the meeting and marriage of a man and woman in the remote future of Day Million. Or it can be *episodic.* The most obviously episodic stories are fantastic voyages, like Homer's *Odyssey* and Stanley G. Weinbaum's "A Martian Odyssey," stories which easily break down into separate sections, each dealing with a marvel or adventure encountered on the journey. A little more subtly, the plot of Forster's "The Machine Stops" is also episodic: Part I follows Vashti, the main character's mother, as she closes out the outside world on her air-rocket trip to visit her son Kuno. Part II deals with Kuno's adventures in the open air above ground. Part III chronicles the demise of the underground city after the machine ceases to function. Often within each episode of an episodic plot there may be some or all of the elements of the classic plot structure: exposition, rising action, suspense, climax, recognition, reversal and resolution.

Another way of analyzing plot is according to what are called plot formulas. We begin to understand what a plot formula is when we notice that many of the stories we read for the first time seem familiar; we feel we have read almost the same story before. More than a repetition of the general pattern of rising action, climax, recognition, reversal and resolution described above, we notice the repetition of more specific patterns of events, like boy meets girl, wins girl, loses girl, regains girl, after which either the story ends or—if it's a tear jerker—boy loses girl again, this time permanently. What we have just described is the plot formula for a love story. A *plot formula* is a pattern of specific events that characterize the plot line of a large number of individual works.

There are a number of kinds of plot formulas and ways to approach them. We might find in certain how-to-write-fiction books something like "fifty sure-fire plots for successful commercial fiction." Or we may discover that some highly formulaic plots are thousands of years old, which would lead us into a special class of formulaic stories called myths, a subject we will look at in more detail in the chapter on Symbol and Myth. Of most interest for our purposes at this point, however, is what John G. Cawelti calls the popular story formula (*Adventure, Mystery, Romance*, Chicago: University of Chicago Press, 1976).

Popular story formulas, unlike mythic patterns, are not universal. Rather they tend to be associated with a particular culture and time. One example, the lost race story, has been discussed in detail by Thomas Clareson ("Lost Lands, Lost Races: A Pagan Princess of Their Very Own," in *Many Futures, Many Worlds,* ed. Clareson, cited in Critical Bibliography). This formula, which flourished from the 1880s to the 1920s, begins as follows: "An explorer, scientist, or naval lieutenant, either by chance or intentional quest, [finds] a lost colony or a lost homeland of some vanished or little-known civilization." This beginning provided a framework for primarily two different kinds of story, utopias and love stories. In utopias the discovered land was used as an inspiration for debate on the burning issues of the day: socialism, the conflict between the advantages of technology and the ideal of closeness to nature, the question of the reconciliation of new discoveries to old religious beliefs (some lost lands turned out to be what was left of the original Eden), and others. In utopian stories, where the center of interest is more on debate over issues than on plot, it is common for writers to choose among the handiest, most popular plots of the time in order to set up debate.

But the most popular use of the lost race story was to extend the plot into a very characteristic and highly formulaic love story: the hero finds and falls in love with a beautiful pagan princess. She is typically voluptuous, her beauty and the isolation and danger of the lost land call forth from the civilized hero powerful urges which most readers today would call natural, but which readers of the late nineteenth and early twentieth centuries considered "primitive." Not only is the hero sexually aroused, but circumstances typically demand that he resort to violent action to rescue or defend the princess (often he first discovers her as she is about to be sacrificed). The tension between civilization and primitivism, the cause of the major conflict experienced by the hero, is typically resolved in one of two ways: the woman tragically dies and he returns sadly to civilization; or they unite in marriage and live happily ever after in the lost land. Rarely do they both return to civilization.

The recognition of a formula such as this is interesting in itself, but it raises some interesting questions, most especially the reason for its popularity. The answer to this question can be important, since formula literature tends to be the most generally popular literature of its time, and formulas, therefore, often tell us something about the popular consciousness of the time. For example, the lost race formula in its characteristic love-story form flourished at a time when Western civilization, at least on the surface, seemed confident, even smug, about its progress, the advances that were seen in new technology and what Westerners thought were "improved" morals. The popularity of the lost race novel, with its emphasis on the lure of the primitive and the erotic, suggests that people may have been less satisfied with "progress" than most were willing to admit. Or perhaps people were satisfied enough with progress but found in fiction like the lost race novel aspects of life in which it was not socially acceptable to participate more overtly.

One could make similar speculations about the popular consciousness reflected in alien encounter stories. The alien encounter story is not itself a formula, but, again, when a large number of such stories exhibit a certain plot pattern during a specific period, we are dealing with a formula. During the 1930s and 1940s the alien encountered was most typically the BEM, the Bug-Eyed-Monster, and the plot revolved around battling and usually destroying the monster. This pattern predominated during a period in which we as a nation were most isolationist and xenophobic, afraid of people of different nationalities, races and religions. Popular story formulas about aliens, in other words, reflected our attitudes toward humans we regarded as aliens.

Another important aspect of formula literature is that, although it is generally seen as inferior, it has frequently provided frameworks which have been used by skilled writers to produce good or even great works. In England around 1600, for instance, a popular stage formula was that of the revenge tragedy, which

Shakespeare used as the basic plot of *Hamlet*. The difference between mere formulas and the *Hamlets* begins with the fact that formulas are cliches which evoke something like conditioned responses. That is, if we read a story with a handsome hero and a beautiful heroine being attacked by a fearsome monster, we do not expect the girl to fall in love with the monster, nor are we likely to expect our own sympathies to shift in favor of the monster against the human hero. If they do, however, if our expectations are violated, such variations or violations of the formula provoke more thoughtful response.

More important to the excellence of a work of fiction than mere alteration of the plot pattern, however, are the ways in which the significance and impact of a story, which may be basically formulaic, are extended and deepened by the skillful development and control of the other elements of fiction like characterization, setting, point of view, language, tone, or symbol. These are elements which will be examined in the following chapters. But for now we can simply add that both a knowledge of the classic plot pattern and a sensitivity to the possibilities of plot formulas can give us valuable insight into what a story is about and what is unique about it.

CHARACTER

The characters of a story are the imaginary persons, whether humans, androids, or aliens from a remote galaxy, who perform the actions that constitute plot. Sometimes the characters' primary value is that they carry out the actions which reveal what happens in the story. In other cases, it may be more important to understand who the characters are and how they change during the story than to simply be aware of what they do. But whether the emphasis is on the actions done or on the characters doing, characters are essential, and a grasp of the ways in which characters may be presented and the importance of the degree to which they are developed can be invaluable.

Methods of Presentation

An author may choose to present characters either directly or indirectly, or, most commonly, by a combination of the two methods. In direct presentation, the author *tells* us about a character through direct exposition, a straightforward explanation, or through comments about a character made by other characters. In indirect presentation, the author *shows* us a character: we infer what the character is from what he does, what he says, and what he thinks.

Direct exposition, the first form of direct presentation, allows the author to provide the reader with important information quickly. Its primary advantage is its economy. Characters may be physically described, their life histories to the time of the story traced, and their attitudes delineated within the space of a paragraph or two; the direct exposition given about Manue Nanti in Walter M. Miller, Jr.'s "Crucifixus Etiam" illustrates how concisely the outlines of a character may be drawn in this way. In the first three paragraphs of the story, we are provided with a physical description of Manue, "a big youth, heavy-boned and built for labor"; an indication of his temperament, "a wistful good humor that helped him to take a lot of guff from whiskey-breathed foremen"; a view of his dream, "to travel, to see the far corners of the world, the strange cultures, the simple people"; and his reason for becoming a laborer on Mars, to "finish his five-year contract with fifty thousand dollars in the bank, return to Earth, and retire at the age of twenty-four."

Since characters, like people, also are defined in part by what others say about them, an author can allow one character to provide us with information about another character. If, for example, Jane Person says that John Person is eccentric, then we as readers begin to watch for signs of eccentricity. This is a second commonly-used method of direct character presentation, and it permits the author to tell us about a character without being present in the narrative and while moving the story's action through dialogue. We may receive facts: a physical description, a life history, an incident, or any of the comments one person might make about another. Sometimes new information explains what might otherwise seem to be an inexplicable alteration in a character's behavior. If a kindly codger, clearly trustworthy, says of hero Trusty, "Oh, he thinks he's a pacifist all right, but he's got a powerful temper when he's roused," we will accept more readily Trusty's later violence, even though he has consistently espoused non-violence. Sometimes additional facts will change our view of a character. When Ellen in Robert Silverberg's "Sundance" makes the comment, "It's only a year and a half since his personality reconstruct, and he had a pretty bad breakdown back then," the information about Tom's mental stability may alter the manner in which we perceive him. Of course, like people, characters are not always reliable: they can be mistaken in their facts, or they can lie. If a character with reason to be jealous of another character begins to spread rumors that seem to be inconsistent with what we already know, we may withhold judgment temporarily, at least until we discover whether or not what has been said may tell us more about the speaker than about the character described.

When an author allows us to infer what a character is by showing us the character speaking or acting, he has used indirect presentation. Indirect presentation may not be as economical as direct presentation, but it is more convincing, and a character must do or say something if a story, rather than a character sketch or an essay, is to be written. We may accept what we are told about a character's ruthlessness, but we find it more emotionally persuasive if we also hear him plan to financially destroy a former friend or watch him stab an opponent with a poison-tipped sword, that is, if he speaks and acts ruthlessly. We could be told that Old Mose in Clifford Simak's "A Death in the House" is fond of his alien visitor: that he gives his carefully-hidden silver to his alien companion to enable it to return to its home planet dramatizes his affection.

The internal monologue, an exploration of the character's thoughts, offers the reader an even greater in-depth knowledge of the character. We may discover more about a character from his or her internal monologue than we know about our best friends: honest reactions to events and people, motivations, confusions, uncertainties and preoccupations. If the author chooses to have a character lie or betray his ideals, the truth will be clear from the internal monologue: the character appears to us unmasked. Some stories are based on a psychological understanding of character that is nearly impossible to achieve without the use of internal monologue. In Robert Silverberg's "Sundance," for example, Tom Two Ribbons loses touch with reality and can no longer be certain whether he is part of a team of scientists studying an alien culture, a murderer exterminating sentient beings as his ancestors, the Sioux, once were exterminated, or an embittered, disturbed man undergoing therapy. If we are to participate in his attempts to find reality, we must enter his mind, and we do so through his internal monologue.

Degree of Development

These methods of presentation should lead us to a sense of a character's relative completeness or incompleteness, or our sense of its *development*. In life, when we meet someone, we may be impressed by one or two traits; as we get to know the individual, we may find out more about him or her. We may learn about a person's conflicts, joys, or sorrows, and if we know the individual over a period of time, we may watch him or her change, adopt new standards and ways of life. We may even become more sympathetic to someone we have previously disliked, or learn to mistrust someone whom we previously thought reliable. In fiction there are many characters whom we will know only by one or two traits; some we will know more deeply, some we will see change as the story progresses, and some we will see remaining the same thoughout the story. The difference between fiction and life is that in fiction the author controls how much information we have about a character he or she wishes us to know.

We understand character development in one or both of two ways: (a) how fully portrayed the characters appear to us within the context of the full story, and (b) how the character changes in time from beginning of the story to the end. When talking of the former aspect of character development, we refer to characters as *flat* or *round*; when talking of the latter, we refer to them as *static* or *dynamic*.

When an author creates a *flat* character, he or she concentrates on one or two dominant traits of a character's personality; by simple description or a few words of dialogue, we recognize the character instantly. If asked to, we could probably summarize the character in a few words or in a sentence.

The opposite of flat is round, of course, and this term, when applied to a character in a story, suggests that he or she is more realized for us than the character described in a few words. When the author delves into the mind of the character—usually by direct exposition and internal monologue—so that we get a more complete picture of his or her mental make-up, we call the character *round*.

It is difficult to talk about character in science fiction without discussing a certain number of types common to the genre that fit into a "flat" character category. We know, for example, what a "spaceman hero" is usually like: young, daring, technically proficient, generally white and male—a type exemplified by Luke Skywalker of the film *Star Wars*. Likewise, the standard alien should be physically grotesque and generally malevolent. The females, if there are any at all, are young, attractive in a conventional way, and subservient to the male heroes. Furthermore, science fiction may use types from other kinds of literature by putting what are essentially detectives, cowboys and sports car drivers in space gear. Needless to say, not all science fiction stories exhibit these *stock characters;* many current writers may omit them altogether. However, because we all, to a certain extent, expect them, an author can make use of our expectations for his or her own purposes, as we will see below.

We often go to certain kinds of science fiction stories expecting stock characters. Our first viewing of a *Star Trek* episode, for example, will establish its characters permanently in our minds; we will expect Captain Kirk, in subsequent shows, to act as an authority figure on the spaceship, and will expect Spock to give advice based on logic and computation of data. If they act otherwise without adequate reason, our expectations will be violated, and we will be confused for no good purpose. It is the interplay of the given characters with the events of the

Star-Trek story that gives the episode its interest.

Sometimes science fiction authors use our expectations about stock characters by showing others in the story reacting to these characters in an unconventional way. One example is Clifford Simak's "A Death in the House," a story about a lonely and eccentric old man who takes care of an alien creature who has come to him. Stories of this sort frequently resemble familiar childhood tales about how an individual comes to know and love something which at first seems repellent, such as an ugly dog, a frog that turns out to be a prince, or a beggar who turns out to be Christ. Unlike these stories, however, the alien does not turn out to be anyone special; it is "a horrid-looking thing, green and shiny, with some purple spots on it," and we learn what it is thinking only at the end of the story. Yet in spite of the creature's strangeness, which in a more conventional story might inspire fear, the old man responds to it sympathetically.

At other times, science fiction authors attempt to reverse our conventional responses to stock characters as a means of exploring unconventional ideas. An example of this is Robert Sheckley's "Specialist," in which the functions of a spaceship are performed not by human beings, but by creatures who in fact form the spaceship itself. The single human member of the crew has been killed in a proton storm, and the ship comes to Earth to look for a new human. These characters, with function-identifying names such as "Eye," "Engine," and "Walls," appear grotesque by any standard. Furthermore, they are flat characters, because Sheckley emphasizes a single dominant trait in each one. However, by showing them working and carousing together, Sheckley attempts to examine the notion of cooperation (as opposed to the non-cooperation of the human race) and by the end of the story has created a sympathy for them and their ideas which is all but impossible for us to feel when we first begin reading the story.

In addition, authors may reverse our conventional

responses by giving characters traits not ordinarily associated with their stock types. Joanna Russ's "When It Changed" does this, again, for the purpose of exploring unconventional ideas. "When It Changed" is about a planet society which has been inhabited only by women for the past 600 years, and which is suddenly disrupted by the visit of four spacemen from Earth. We might expect these women to be gushing with enthusiasm over the arrival of these supposedly competent, handsome men, but they are not; they feel instead that these strange, ugly creatures will destroy the good society they have created. The men, in fact, are ignorant and foolish; they are unable to shake off past prejudices and have damaged their own society. Russ's characterization of the males is more "flat" than that of the females; the women in her story are complicated, interesting people. This in itself is a reversal of the usual pattern of the male-figure dominated science fiction story, and Russ's tale is a kind of critique of that story, as well as a critique of the attitudes toward women on which such a story is based.

In fact, the male characters of "When It Changed" function primarily as *foils*—characters who serve to highlight, by contrast, the views or personalities of other characters in a story. Foils are found everywhere in literature, as well as in other forms of entertainment; for example, the straight man in comedy teams, such as Bud Abbott of Abbott and Costello, and Dan Rowan of Rowan and Martin, frequently functions as the foil; so does the comical side-kick in Westerns, whom actors like Gabby Hayes, Walter Brennan and Andy Devine have often played. Foils are frequently—but not always—flat characters because, although they may be interesting in themselves, their purpose is to highlight or reflect (which is why they are called foils) other characters.

A flat character, like a foil or some of the other characters mentioned above, is not necessarily a stock character. Nevertheless, just as no person is completely individual, no character is completely unique; all characters in fiction contain stock elements. If they did not, we could not understand them. Likewise, a stock character does not necessarily have to be flat; a hero who is brave and virtuous may commit or wish to commit an evil act, or a heroine may show a streak of independence.

The relation between flat and round may be better understood not by thinking of these two terms as two vast file drawers into which all the characters of fiction may be placed, but rather as two opposite poles of a continuum. The alien in "A Death in the House" is almost completely flat; we do not even know what it is thinking until we are presented with the expository material at the end of the story. On the other hand, the central character of "When It Changed" is round; as she narrates the story, we get to know her because she tells us what is going on in her mind as she interacts with other characters in the story. We learn her history, hopes, interests and fears, and as we do, it becomes harder to summarize her character in a few words or a sentence. Tom Two Ribbons of "Sundance" is likewise a round character, because large portions of the story are told from the point of view of his perhaps disordered mind, and we learn of his conflicts from this internal monologue.

Science fiction has often been criticized for its lack of complex characters, or, in other words, for its preponderance of flat characters. It is quite true that the characters in science fiction lack the depth of, for example, the central characters in two major modern works of fiction, James Joyce's *Ulysses* and Marcel Proust's *Remembrance of Things Past*. We must remember, however, that frequently the purpose of a science fiction story is not to explore the consciousness of a particular individual, but to examine an idea or create a sense of wonder at the immensity and the vast possibilities of the Universe. In either case, complex characterization would distract from the purpose of such a story. As the fantasy writer C.S. Lewis wrote, "Every good writer knows that the more unusual the scenes and events of his story are, the slighter, the more ordinary, the more typical his persons should be" ("On Science Fiction," in Lewis' *Of Other Worlds,* cited in Critical Bibliography).

The second way of seeing character development is the relative change of character through time. Characters may be either *static*—they do not change—or *dynamic*—they do change. To return to the *Star Trek* example given earlier, we may, as we watch more programs, be given more information about the past lives of the major characters and know the past affects their present ways of life; but we do not see Kirk or Spock, for instance, change after the end of each program. Even though they may learn something during the course of an episode, they remain essentially the same persons at the end. Thus, we call them static.

Like flat characters, static characters in science fiction have many uses. All of the flat, stock characters mentioned above are basically static; nevertheless, a character who never changes does not have to be a flat character. It was noted above that the narrator of Russ's "When It Changed" is relatively round, but we do not see her change sustantially in the story.

"Change" in this context—in fact, in the context of most fiction—means that the character, as the result of experiencing events and interacting with other characters in a story, comes to a new understanding either of self, the universe, or the nature of good and evil. A character may change into a dog, or may change jobs, but this means nothing unless it is accompanied by a change in his or her outlook. Sometimes the new understanding can be a realization that things are confusing—that the world is a meaningless blur of events; sometimes the new understanding may be mistaken or false, at least from our viewpoint as readers—but it is still a development in time. This new understanding may be tied to a real or potential behavior change in the character, but it does not necessarily have to be so tied. The character who changes in this sense is called dynamic.

A good example of a dynamic character is Manue Nanti in "Crucifixus Etiam," by Walter Miller, Jr. Manue comes to Mars to work on a project that will some day make the planet inhabitable for human beings. The working conditions are unjust and ultimatley crippling, and the job he is doing, because it offers no immediate results and is destroying his lungs, appears meaningless. Yet when the brutalized workforce of the planet almost begins a rebellion, Manue strikes down its leader, and realizes that his work is not an exercise in cruelty but a glorious adventure in civilization-building on Mars, the "eight-century passion of human faith in the destiny of the race of Man." Manue is substantially different at the end of the story.

Because the author of "Crucifixus Etiam" gives us Manue's thoughts and exposes us to his sharp internal conflicts, Manue is also a "round" character. However, just as a static character does not have to be flat, a dynamic character does not have to be round. Mose in "A Death in the House" is close to being a completely flat character; we are not given a great deal of psychological information about him, and he acts mostly according to our stock conception of an eccentric old codger. However, because Mose offers the alien money from his hoard, he indicates that he has at least a glimmer of understanding of the value of friendship that he did not have when the story opened. It should also be noted that the concepts static and dynamic, like flat and round, may be seen as poles on a continuum. A character such as Mose, for example, while not completely static, is not as dynamic as a character such as Manue Nanti, whose change is more fully portrayed.

As many writers have pointed out, characterization is interwoven with point of view, the action, and the language of a story. However, by isolating—somewhat artificially, it may be admitted—methods of presentation and types and degree of character development, we may see how an author creates characters who are both memorable to us and who contribute to the ultimate meaning of the story.

SETTING

Setting commonly refers to the place and time in which action occurs within a story. It is a concept which many readers wrongly associate only with words like "description" or "exposition," but it is an important part of a story, and the expense of some attention and patience on it can be rewarding. This is especially true with science fiction, where setting can be the most important element in a story.

There are three approaches to setting which we shall consider in the following discussion, all of which are closely related to each other: what kinds of setting we may find in fiction, how setting is established, and how setting functions in or contributes to a story.

The Kinds of Setting

Setting in science fiction is especially rich because of its combination of characteristics associated with two strongly contrasting literary modes, romance and realism. The romance, associated with medieval tales of knightly deeds, is a mode of fiction characterized by its remoteness from the scenes and incidents of everyday life; its settings include supernatural and mythological worlds inhabited by monsters, faeries and heroes who ride enchanted steeds and wield magic swords. Realism, on the other hand, is characterized by its closeness to the phenomena of everyday life; its settings are as familiar to us as our own homes and cities, and if less familiar, they are kinds of places depicted in ways that we know we could verify if we chose to travel there. Science fiction most typically combines these two modes by making use of settings remote in time and space and at the same time establishing connections with our own world based on modern science and depicting that remote world in a more or less scientific manner. That is, the setting may be a starship or distant planet, but each setting is presented so that we feel that when starships are made, they may really be like this, and if we could travel to distant planets, we might find one like this one.

The degree to which such settings convince us may vary considerably, however, since science fiction mixes romance and realism in varying proportions. We can therefore represent the varieties of science fiction settings by thinking of the whole of science fiction as a spectrum with opposite ends labeled romance and realism. Science fiction with the most realistic settings would take place in what seems to be our everyday world, but that world would be altered by an intrusion from the remote, from something outside our normal realm of experience: a near miss by a wandering heavenly body as in H.G. Wells' "The Star," an atomic war as in Robert Merle's *Malevil,* a biological disaster as in John Christopher's *No Blade of Grass.* At the opposite end of the spectrum would be worlds far from our own in which the settings and props of future technologies and new discoveries are used as though they were faery lands, enchanted castles and magic swords. Such is the case with the scientific romances of Edgar Rice Burroughs, the space opera of E.E. Smith's Skylark and Lensman series, the old movie serials and comic strips like *Buck Rogers* and *Flash Gordon,* and the recently popular film *Star Wars.*

As these examples may have suggested to you, the opposite ends of our spectrum are not absolutely distinct. At the romance end of the spectrum a story may be called science fiction because of only the slightest element of realistic possibility, like the fact that we journey on a rocket ship instead of a magic carpet. At the realistic end of the spectrum, an intruding element like a nuclear war is certainly not very remote, but it does represent some element of romance: the world is at least minimally altered by some condition, however probable, not yet acting in the world. A story written in the 1970s, for example, set in a lab where new and deadly viruses are being created, could simply be realistic fiction. If the story told of an escape of the virus and a resultant plague (assuming that hasn't happened already), it would be at least minimal science fiction.

Notice also that the historical context of a story can determine whether or not we are dealing with a science fiction setting. If the story set in the lab described above had been written in 1890, with only the threat of escaping virus included, it would still clearly be science fiction. A similar case is Lester del Rey's *Nerves,* a story about a near disaster from an accident in a nuclear energy plant— it was first published in 1942, when atom bombs didn't exist, much less controlled nuclear reactors.

Within these limits there is an almost infinite variety of possibilities for setting. The sources of remoteness are obvious enough: scientific or technological breakthrough, space travel, alien cultures, evolutionary changes, time travel, parallel worlds. The sources of realism, however, are more complex, and the means by which connections with our own world are established, the ways in which sf makes its worlds believable, even plausible, require more discussion.

The Establishment of Setting

An effective setting is something far easier to appreciate than to create. It involves the presentation of carefully selected details through a mixture of exposition, dialogue and action. The detail selected includes obvious elements like the land or streets and their various vegetations, the characters' dwellings, furnishings, clothing, and diet, their implements, tools and customs. It can also include the religious, social and political events in the story. It can even include the language of characters: a writer with no ear for language variations could probably not convincingly tell a story set in Harlem, the southern or southwestern United States, or King Arthur's England, no matter how thoroughly he knew the physical details of the setting.

For science fiction the most characteristic means of establishing a believable setting is a technique called extrapolation, a term derived from mathematics and engineering. If, for example, we can plot the behavior of an object, process, or function over a known period of time or range of temperature, and if our observations reveal a regular pattern of change, then we can *extrapolate,* extend our picture of the pattern of change beyond our data. A practical example would be the fact that an astronomer, on the basis of the last hundred years or so of observations, can quite accurately describe how the sky will look two thousand years from now or how it must have looked to a shepherd on the night of Christ's birth. As you may know, this is the principle behind the design of planetariums.

As applied to future studies, extrapolation means a more or less rigorous attempt to work out the details of a future world on the basis of observations of history and current tendencies. We say "more or less rigorous" because extrapolation can vary from the highly probable—in what position we will see Venus tomorrow night—to the highly speculative—the most common form of transportation two hundred years from now (it could be ox cart). Its validity and the extent to which it can be carried beyond known data depend both on the accuracy and completeness of observations of past and present and on the assumption that no new or unanticipated variables will be introduced into the equation. And, of course, the variables involved in the development of human culture and society are considerably more complex than those of astronomy. Nevertheless, extrapolation has in recent years become an important part of the science of statistics and has been applied to the new science of future studies.

One of the best examples of this is a book called *The Limits of Growth* (by Donella H. Meadows, Dennis L. Meadows, Jorgen Randers, William W. Behrens III, New York: Universe Books, 1972). In this book a group of researchers worked out a world model with the help of a computer. In one series of studies they considered five variables—natural resources, food per capita, population, industrial output per capita and pollution—and plotted the growth curves for each interacting with the others for the period from 1900 to 2100. Everything beyond around 1970 was, of course, extrapolated, and a whole series of extrapolations was worked out on the basis of various combinations of assumptions. Suppose, for example, nuclear power is developed, effectively doubling resource reserves and making possible extensive recycling programs; what happens to population, pollution and all the others? The results are interesting and disturbing and have already been exploited by science fiction writers to help them establish credible settings.

But whether created with the aid of computers or with the unaided human imagination, the concept of a world model is central to the kind of extrapolation characteristic of science fiction. It presents a fictional model of what the world, or some portion of it, might be, under certain crucial conditions not existing at present.

How elaborate that model appears in a given story, however, may vary considerably. Imagine a plot set in the year 2100. One writer may spend many words explaining to his 1970s audience conditions current in 2100 and how they got to be that way. Another writer may simply present the story as though it were a realistic novel *written* in 2100, spending no more time explaining Neo-Unionists or the long-range frammis than a writer today would spend explaining Democrats or the telephone. Both writers may have exerted the same effort working out the details of their models, but each selects differently when he or she makes the decisions about which details will be presented and in what manner. Those decisions are based

on the writer's sense of what the story as a whole is doing
and how he can best use setting to reinforce that purpose.

The Function of Setting

How extrapolation is applied in establishing setting
depends largely on how the author wants setting to
function in the story. There are innumerable ways in
which setting can function, but a brief discussion of some
of the more common ones can give us an idea of the
variation we are likely to find.

Perhaps the most obvious type of extrapolative story
is one which isolates some particular problem or evil in
present-day society and projects it into the future. Such
stories usually imply the warning, "If this goes on," and
are exemplified in such classics as E.M. Forster's "The
Machine Stops," Aldous Huxley's *Brave New World,*
George Orwell's *1984*, Frederik Pohl and C.M.
Kornbluth's *The Space Merchants,* and John Brunner's
The Sheep Look Up. Optimistic extrapolations tend to
produce what is called *utopian fantasy* (from the Greek
topos, "place," with a pun on *eu,* "good" and *ou,* "no"),
portraits of ideal social and political orders. These are
exemplified by a more ancient line of works, from Plato's
Republic through Francis Bacon's *The New Atlantis* up to
Edward Bellamy's *Looking Backward* and B.F. Skinner's
Walden Two. Utopian fiction inspires debate among
readers as to whether the ideal model, the supposedly
good place, is really likely to satisfy everyone and whether
we can achieve such a state. A third more complex
alternative, called *utopian satire,* attacks the author's
contemporary society by creating imaginary lands which
contain a mixture of both types. In works like Thomas
More's *Utopia* or Jonathan Swift's *Gulliver's Travels* we
may find in one scene a comic exaggeration of a
contemporary problem and in another an ideal solution to
a different problem. Swift satirizes England's religious
divisions by having Gulliver describe a controversy
among the diminutive Lilliputians between the Big-

Endians and the Little-Endians, sects which disagree on the proper way to break an egg. The gigantic Brobdingnagians, on the other hand, are models of philosophical common sense, since their learning "consists only in morality, history, poetry, and mathematics," the last of which is "wholly applied to what may be useful in life," while Gulliver is unable to get them to understand the first thing about contemporary preoccupations like "entities, abstractions, and transcendentals."

In all three types, whether utopia, utopian satire, or *dystopia* ("a bad place," a word created about twenty-five years ago as a result of science fiction), the importance of setting is indicated by the fact that the setting itself raises questions central to the story's theme, and all three types direct us to critical examination of our own present.

All science fiction, however, cannot be classified as variations of utopia. In many highly extrapolative stories the new world is neither particularly good nor bad. When Robert A. Heinlein wrote "The Roads Must Roll" in 1940, for instance, he speculated that this country would soon abandon the inefficient, dangerous, individually-owned automobile and construct instead a vast network of moving roads, functioning something like giant conveyer belts. (In fact, we rejected any efficient system of mass transit and instead encouraged automobiles by constructing a vast network of state and interstate highways—we might well have paid closer attention to Heinlein.) In the story the result of the moving roads is improved transportation, but by no means an ideal social order, and Heinlein's plot focuses on the problem of how the roads would have to be managed to prevent dissident minorities from blackmailing the country by stopping key roads (a situation which anticipated the problem of airline highjacking). Thus in the Heinlein story, setting becomes a means of exploring the consequences of a particular technological development. Such stories are usually described in the more neutral terms of "What if" rather than "If this goes on" (dystopia) or "If only we could" (utopia).

In all these story types the emphasis on setting can vary considerably. Some utopias, for instance, are almost all description and analysis of setting, and there is little plot. Dystopias tend to exhibit more plot, but setting, insofar as it expresses the evil system which dominates society, can become almost a character itself, as in J.G. Ballard's "The Subliminal Man," where setting, more than any living person in the story, functions as the enemy. The greatest variety of setting, however, is to be found in the "What if" story, where extrapolation can be more speculative and imaginative. Future settings can be based on developments which go beyond the possibilities inherent in current science: we may find in such fiction faster-than-light drives, electronic transporter mechanism, androids, exotic alien creatures and planets, parallel worlds, time travel, telepathy or teleportation. In spite of the varying remoteness of such developments, however, all offer numerous possibilities for establishing or playing off connections with our own world.

Such connections begin with the fact that modern sciences like nuclear physics, genetics, astronomy and paleontology have all revealed that certain settings which seem remote are parts of actual existence. An experience which many writers and readers consider central to science fiction, the sense of wonder, is often evoked by fundamental parts of our real setting, like the vast expanses of space and time which surround us and of which our own existence is an inconceivably small part. Arthur C. Clarke's "The Sentinel" brings us to a realization of such vastness by starting with a carefully extrapolated moon base; near the base an object is discovered which leads to the revelation of a visit to our solar system by an incredibly advanced culture billions of years ago. How far advanced must they be now? Some science fiction writers create an expanded sense of time by building whole cycles of stories around carefully elaborated future histories. Clifford Simak's *City* is a series of related short stories which reveal a future history covering thousands of years. Nearly all of Cordwainer Smith's stories fit into an elaborate future history covering tens of thousands of years. And all such elaborations are to some degree indebted to Olaf Stapledon, a British philosopher who presented in his *Last and First Men* (1930) not so much a novel as a fictional history of the next two billion years.

Such complex settings are based not only on the sense of the vastness of space and time but also on the sense of cause and consequence revealed by history. A colony planet can become the setting for a reexamination of the American colonial experience as in Philip Jose Farmer's *Dare*—or of the Vietnamese colonial experience as in Ursula Le Guin's *The Word for World is Forest*. A galactic empire can disintegrate in another version of the fall of Rome, as in Isaac Asimov's Foundation trilogy, or a new religious and military force can emerge in a variation on the rise of Islam, as in Frank Herbert's *Dune*.

Combinations of historical precedent and extrapolation have also produced some highly conventionalized settings. Stories of galactic conflict, for example, are often set in spaceships that are adaptations of more familiar submarines or bombers; the shipboard setting of the Star Trek series is essentially a battleship, complete with bridge, engine room, crew's quarters, sick bay, bulkheads, yeomen, and so forth. Essential variations of the old patterns, like shuttle craft, transporters, photon torpedoes, and "Ahead Warp factor I" instead of landing craft, helicopters, depth charges, and "All engines ahead standard," are all well established science fiction conventions. These similarities do not necessarily imply, however, that such settings are weak. Science fiction settings are usually mixtures of the familiar and the unfamiliar, the conventional and the original. Their effectivenes may depend less on the accuracy of their major premises than on the quality of the detail selected, the skill with which it is presented and purpose which the setting serves.

Other disciplines can influence extrapolation as well. Prehistoric settings like that of William Golding's *The Inheritors* can be extrapolated from a mixture of archeology (the study of artifacts of the ancient past) and anthropology (the study of the full range of human cultures). Archeology can as well become the basis for a setting of the far future, as in Arthur C. Clarke's "History Lesson," in which alien explorers land on Earth tens of thousands of years from now and discover evidence of the existence of a long extinct sentient race: ours. It turns out that the primary artifact they use to reconstruct the culture of the lost race is a reel of film, a Donald Duck cartoon. Anthropology is often an aid to the establishment of alien settings, many of which are based on human cultures alien only to Western man. Roger Zelazny's Mars in "A Rose for Ecclesiastes," for example, may be examined in comparison to Hindu culture.

Setting can also help present or define fundamental problems or ideas which a story explores. Clarke's "The Sentinel," in expanding our sense of space and time, also raises questions about man's place and relative importance in the universe. Settings based on historical precedent like Asimov's Foundation series or Herbert's *Dune* provide the basis for speculations about human freedom and the extent to which individual lives are determined by external conditions. Speculations about human destiny and the limits of our knowledge and growth are also central to stories about the next evolutionary steps humanity is likely to pass through. Theodore Sturgeon's *More than Human* and Clarke's *Childhood's End* both deal with changes in man and the world which are likely to follow from such steps.

Any study of mankind's environment is intimately related to the study of man himself, since that environment both shapes and is shaped by him and reflects the nature of his consciousness. There are not only, therefore, extrapolative and philosophical dimensions to setting, but also psychological dimensions. Elements of setting may be used to complement or to contrast with the emotional state of the character: a joyful person can find his cheerfulness reflected by a sunny day; an unhappy person can be further depressed by the same beautiful day; we may repeatedly find an unenlightened person in literally dark places; a character spiritually lost may be presented as literally lost in a jungle or a desert— or if the same character lives in a city, that city may be described in terms which suggest a jungle or a desert. (We will see more about the effects and purposes of describing one thing in terms of another in the chapter on Language, especially the subsection, Imagery and Figurative Language.)

Science fiction offers the opportunity to express and explore these kinds of relationships more explicitly than conventional realistic fiction. The city described above can literally become a jungle or desert, given sufficient time or disaster, as it does in Stephen Vincent Benet's "By the Waters of Babylon." Other planets, like Jupiter in Simak's "Desertion" (one of the stories from *City*) or the alien planet in Ray Bradbury's "Here There Be Tygers," are less extrapolations than imaginative leaps into lands of heart's desire where man's wishes are rendered possible. In Simak's story a man changed into a Jovian life form finds himself so perfectly adapted to his new environment that all conflict between man and nature disappears; he becomes united with nature and absorbed in its beauty to a degree that man can only imagine as having existed in Eden. In Bradbury's story a character discovers another version of union with nature, only in this case a whole planet turns out to be a single sentient creature, feminine in nature, with whom the man discovers a loving relationship. Ingeniously Bradbury manages to use setting to explore both ecological and sexual problems and to show the relationship between the two. Such worlds can express not only our dreams, but also our nightmares; indeed they can be used as imaginative projections of an infinite variety of states of consciousness. In Bradbury's "The Veldt," for instance, a special nursery room designed to create moving three dimensional images of whatever the occupants desire permits two spoiled children to create an image of a sweltering African veldt with hungry lions. The parents realize too late that the savage setting reflects the children's attitude toward the parents, who become the actual victims of their children's murderous fantasies. Setting thus becomes an important basis for a study in child psychology. Philip Dick writes a number of stories in which consciousness altering drugs become the means of changing not only people's sense of the world but the world itself. Such examples can only hint at the variety of ways in which setting can function in science fiction as a means of exploring inner as well as outer space.

The more setting reflects inner space, the further we move from extrapolative realism and the closer we approach the symbolic techniques of romance (the nature of symbols and their applications to setting are discussed in more detail in chapter ten, Symbol and Myth). But one end of our spectrum from realism to romance is not inherently preferable to the other, nor more true. A successful setting works not necessarily because it is true in any literal sense nor because it turns out to be accurate prophecy, but because the author makes it seem true while we are within the story—and perhaps also because that setting has altered our way of looking at our own world. A special characteristic of science fiction is that its use of various kinds of extrapolation forms a basis for heightening the sense of reality in settings which can exhibit an infinite variety of differences from and ways of commenting on the everyday world we know.

POINT OF VIEW

Once an author has chosen his characters and setting and worked out his plot outline, he still has a decision to make which can radically affect the way we respond to the story: Who is going to tell it? Through whose eyes will we see the events unfold? How crucial this choice is can be suggested by imagining how different a hackneyed plot with stock hero, heroine and villain might be if it were told by the villain. The general term applied to this question of the position or positions from which we see the action and characters of a story is *point of view*.

Point of view is a term which has a number of other applications, one of which can sometimes cause confusion. We can speak of any person's or character's point of view in the general sense of the *way* in which he or she looks at events and characters. In this chapter, however, we will use point of view in the technical sense in which it refers to a narrative strategy deliberately chosen by the author by means of which the reader is set up to view the story unfolding from a particular perspective.

Because point of view concerns the question of what person is telling the story, it has become customary to divide the possible choices into broad categories according to the classifications provided by the personal pronouns. If the narrator refers to himself as "I" and tells a story of his personal experiences, the point of view is *first person;* if all characters are described by the narrator with pronouns like "he," "she," "it," "they," the point of view is *third person.* Within these broad categories, however, we can find an enormous variety of possibilities.

First Person

In the first person narrative the narrator is directly involved in plot by being a character in the story. This choice is often used for fictionalized travel narratives like *Gulliver's Travels,* where Jonathan Swift wants to create the sense of authenticity which an eye witness account can provide. He therefore has Gulliver tell his own story. First person can also be effective in a situation where the author wants to present a highly self-conscious and introspective character examining his own feelings, as in Robert Silverberg's *Dying Inside.* Told by the main character, a telepath, the story examines the loneliness and agony experienced by a person with peculiar insight into human cruelty and hypocrisy because he always knows what people are really thinking.

Two examples as different as these should suggest something of the range of possible effects offered by first person point of view. These effects can be varied not only by the kinds of events presented—travels to strange places or introspection—but by the degree of the narrator's closeness to the main action and the kind of character or personality he is.

Often the first person narrator is the major character in the plot, in which case he or she is as close as possible to the main action. But sometimes it is more effective for the narrator to be somewhat removed from the main action by making him or her a secondary character. In the case of the Sherlock Holmes stories, the choice of Dr. Watson as narrator permits the author to place more emphasis on Holmes' extraordinary talents and also doubles the suspense, since Watson is not only vainly trying to solve the crime himself, but just as vainly trying to guess how Holmes is solving it. And Watson's character—his admiration of Holmes, his honest bafflement, his kindness—is part of what engages and holds our interest in the story.

Watson, of course, is a relatively static character, but interesting effects can be produced when the narrator is

58

dynamic, when, through his involvement in the action, he grows or otherwise changes so that the reader's understanding of the situation changes with him or her. This effect is accomplished to an extreme degree through the device of Charlie Gordon's "progress reports" in Daniel Keyes' "Flowers for Algernon." The reader senses the changes in Charlie as he grows from a mental retardate pathetically wishing he could be smart like everyone else—"They said Miss Kinnian told that I was her bestist pupil in the adult nite scool becaus I tried the hardist and I reely wantid to lern"—to a scientific genius appalled at the ignorance of the neurosurgeon who had altered his intelligence—"I was shocked to learn that the only ancient languages he could read were Latin, Greek, and Hebrew, and that he knows almost nothing of mathematics beyond the elementary levels of the calculus of variations."

Interesting complications are also introduced if the narrator is not a trustworthy source of information. Sometimes the narrator reveals biases and limitations that make it necessary for the reader to deduce that the truth of a situation is other than what the narrator says it is. This variation of first person point of view is called the *unreliable narrator*. In "Eyebem" Gene Wolfe tells a story about the limitations of robots, but he does so by having the robot tell his own story. At first we sympathize with Eyebem's insecure sense of being a race apart, but as he gains confidence in his superiority to human beings, we begin to question his beliefs. At the end of the story he is approaching electronic death, the erasure of his tapes, and we hear him complain,

We are the advance of the future, not you men. All your stupid human history has been just your own replacement by us, and there's nothing, not one thing, that you can do that we can't do better. Why don't you help me?

The contradiction here between his grand claims of power

and his plea for help reveals his false pride and the unreliability of his judgments.

Finally, a first-person narrator's closeness to the action may be varied according to his position in time with respect to the action. We may, for example, be made aware of the fact that the narrator has completed the action of the story and is telling it to us or reporting it to the proper authority after the fact. He may thus hint at events to come or otherwise make us aware of himself as story teller, controlling suspense by withholding information he knows "now" but did not know "then." Or the author may try for a more natural sense of immediacy by the device of the journal. The narrator is keeping a journal or writing daily progress reports like Charlie Gordon or corresponding nightly to a friend. Thus at the time of writing he knows no more than he presents to us. And sometimes the technique will fall somewhere in between these extremes: the narrator will describe events as happening in the past but will simply make no reference whatever to his present condition. This last choice may seem the least "natural," but it represents a well established convention which most readers are able to accept without losing any sense of suspense. When Edgar Rice Burroughs' John Carter tells his adventures, we not only accept the fact that as adventurer Carter could not have known "then" that a Martian banth with slavering jaws was just around the next bend in the canyon; but we accept the fact that as narrator Carter gives us no warning beforehand, and we may even forget that in order to be the narrator he must have survived the encounter.

Third Person

The third person narrator exists outside the action of the story and may be capable of reporting on a wide variety of kinds of events, internal or external. The most comprehensive kind of third person narrator is the *omniscient author,* who knows everything, who can report actions and dialogue lightyears apart, and who can summarize the thoughts or quote the interior monologue of any character, including non-human entities. For example, the narrator of Clarke's "History Lesson" begins with a focus on the thoughts of Shann, the leader of a tribal remnant of the declining race of man, civilization having been destroyed by a new ice age. Next we see Shann's descendants hiding a collection of precious relics of the civilized past; then we see the final onslaught of the glaciers, and finally the arrival five thousand years later of a Venusian spacecraft, whose occupants are excited but perplexed by their discovery of a film strip which they assume reveals the identity of the past inhabitants of Earth. The third person omniscient narrator here moves from a focus on the individual to the tribe, to nature, and in the end to the thoughts and speculations of aliens. The omniscient narrator can thus quite literally present anything he wishes us to know.

But though the omniscient narrator knows all, he does not tell all. Indeed, he may control the pace or impact of the story by withholding crucial information. In "History Lesson" we are told fairly early in the story that among the precious relics was included "a flat, circular tin, wide in comparison with its depth," which was "heavily sealed, and rattled when shaken." We learn more about the contents of the tin when the Venusians open it, discover a film, and project it. The narrator describes the result to some extent, but as it looked to the Venusians. The actions of the creatures on the film seem almost as puzzling to us as to the Venusians—until the final line of the story, when we are permitted to see the credit line and read what is indecipherable to the aliens: "A Walt Disney Production." Suddenly other clues, like the previous mention of "the little biped...with its characteristic expression of arrogant bad temper," come together, and we realize that this creature, which "for the rest of time...would symbolize the human race," is most probably Donald Duck. Thus the omniscient narrator's control of when we are told crucial information can set up the joke and create the surprise ending.

You will notice that throughout this discussion of third person point of view, we have consistently used the word "narrator" rather than "author" to refer to the storyteller. This has been deliberate, because the third person narrator is never the author himself. (It should be obvious that a first person narrator can never be the author; if he were, the work would be autobiography, not fiction.) However close the narrator may seem to the author, he is more accurately seen as a kind of stage personality, a role assumed for the purpose of effective presentation of the story. The author may assume, for instance, the role of the impersonal historian, as Clarke does in "History Lesson." In order to emphasize this distinction between the narrator's role and the author himself, it is conventional to speak of such a role as a *mask* or *persona*.

The use of a persona is especially clear in a special class of omniscient author point of view, what is called the *intrusive author*. Whereas in most varieties of third person point of view, we are not made strongly aware of the narrator's persona, sometimes, in the variation called intrusive author, the narrator, while giving himself no part in the plot, freely discusses the work with the reader and speaks in his avowed capacity as story teller. He may discuss characters, events, questions of technique or theme, as they arise, presenting his own opinions or wondering aloud how he will make things turn out.

Frederik Pohl uses the intrusive author point of view in "Day Million," a love story of some ten thousand years from now. But it is a story about a boy who was not really a boy—"because he was a hundred and eighty-seven years old"—and a girl who was not really a girl—because "she was a boy." Speaking as intrusive author, the narrator or persona addresses the reader directly: "How angrily you recoil from the page! You say, who the hell wants to read about a pair of queers? Calm yourself. Here are no hot-breathing secrets of perversion for the coterie trade. In fact, if you were to see this girl you would not guess that she was in any sense a boy." The narrator goes on throughout the story deliberately and directly ridiculing the reader for his cultural and temporal enthnocentrism, demanding sympathy and tolerance for his bizarre lovers, and concluding with the question, "Tell me, just how the hell do you think you would look to Tiglath-Pileser, say, or Attila the Hun?"

Further variations of the third person point of view are possible, depending on how the author wishes to limit his point of view, how he chooses to establish the rules of the game and for what effect. These variations are usually referred to as *third person limited*. He may wish to create a more subjective effect by presenting to us all the thoughts and reactions of only one character and presenting all other events as seen from the outside of this character, who is often referred to as the *center of consciousness*. The reader knows what has happened and can make judgments only as the center of consciousness character becomes aware of the situation. The use of this technique, like first person narrative, has some advantages for leading the reader to identify with a particular character and makes it more natural for the author to withhold matters that would destroy suspense— what is told is only what that character alone could know. The reader of Simak's "Desertion," for instance, knows only the questions in the anxious mind of Fowler as volunteer after volunteer disappears into the alien atmosphere outside man's fortress dome on Jupiter. It is not until Fowler himself enters the Jovian atmosphere in the adapted Loper form that he and the reader realize why the volunteers never returned. We can also discover effects with this technique much like those of the first person unreliable narrator if the center of consciousness is a flawed personality. We may at first sympathize with him and see events his way, until we discover his defects and realize the contrast between his perceptions and interpretations and alternative ways of understanding the same events, and if the character is dynamic we may change with him.

For another variation, the author might wish to create a sense of greater objectivity by using the *third person camera* point of view. Here information is limited to external events and dialogue. No character's thoughts or narrator's judgments are presented, and the point of view is detached and impersonal, as though we were looking through the unwinking and unreflective eye of a camera. This is a technique made famous by Ernest Hemingway in his story "The Killers," but writers seem to have found this technique so severely limiting that other examples are rare. Another variation of the type is the pseudo-documentary, like Lawrence Sanders' *The Anderson Tapes*. It is important to remember, however, that, just as with real documentaries, the sense of objective truth created by these techniques is largely an illusion. Even detachment can be a mask, and behind the cold eye of the camera, the author, like a director, is staging the scenes, deciding what we will see, controlling our responses.

Mixed or Shifting Point of View

An author need not limit his choices to a simple decision whether to present his story as the autobiography of one of his characters or to employ one of the variations of the third person. Many pieces of fiction successfully employ what may be called shifting or mixed points of view. One time-honored example is the use of several first person narrators, each of whom tells some part of the story as he or she sees it. Historians of fiction will at once recall the epistolary novel, so popular in the eighteenth century, a novel told through a series of letters written by several characters. A very pertinent example, though it uses only one letter-writer, is that very famous early nineteenth century work of science fiction, Mary Shelley's *Frankenstein, or The Modern Prometheus*. It begins with letters written to his sister by one Robert Walton, a polar explorer, who relates events leading to his encounter with Dr. Frankenstein. The greater part of the novel consists of Frankenstein's own story, which Walton sets down "as nearly as possible in [Frankenstein's] own words," so that Walton seems to disappear. The conclusion returns us to Walton, who narrates as he sees them the events immediately leading up to Frankenstein's fatal, last confrontation with his monster. And finally, having discovered the monster standing over the slain doctor, Walton is able to quote the monster's own version of the tragic story.

The mixture of points of view here is not at all arbitrary. For such a bizarre story, Shelley needed to establish a sober, trustworthy observer-reporter like Walton. The major purpose of the novel was to explore the consciousness of the modern Prometheus, the ironic bringer of the light of forbidden knowledge. For this she needed Frankenstein's own point of view. Finally, the monster tells his tale remorsefully and judges Frankenstein sympathetically, which is far more convincing coming from the doctor's major victim than it would be coming from someone else.

But it is not necessary that shifts in point of view be limited to the same person. It is quite possible for part of a narrative to be written in the first person, part in the third person. A first person narrator begins Jorge Luis Borges' "The House of Asterion" by revealing his preoccupations with the passages and rooms of his house, with his occasional visitors, and with the prophecy that a redeemer will one day deliver him; but he does not reveal his identity. In the final paragraphs the point of view effectively shifts to the third person:

The morning sun reverberated from the bronze sword. There was no longer even a vestige of blood.
"Would you believe it, Ariadne?" said Theseus. "The Minotaur scarcely defended himself."

Ursula Le Guin presents another kind of mixture in *The Left Hand of Darkness.* The bulk of the novel consists of the first person narratives of the two major characters, the after-the-fact narrative of Genly Ai, the lone ambassador to an alien planet, and the journal of Estraven, an important native of the planet. Genly's narrative, which dominates the first third of the novel, leads us at first to share his earlier biases and misconceptions, but as the novel progresses, Estraven's journal and Genly's own growth in understanding lead us to see the situation more truly, and—since his biases and misunderstandings are likely to be close to our own—to grow in understanding of ourselves with Genly. Interspersed among these narratives and making up separate chapters are a first person report of a previous investigator of the planet and various third person narratives of myths and folktales indigenous to the planet.

Robert Silverberg's "Sundance" begins with the rarely used second person, "Today you liquidated about 50,000 Eaters in Sector A, and now you are spending an uneasy night." The "you" of this section, Tom Two Ribbons, becomes "he" in the next section as the point of view shifts to third person, centering on Tom's consciousness. The third section shifts to first person, with Tom speaking: "I noticed something strange today." There follow a series of shifts, including a short section of third person camera focusing on a scene outside Tom's consciousness; it records a conversation in which a character says, "It's only a year and a half since [Tom's] personality reconstruct, and he had a pretty bad breakdown back then." Thus we know we have to contend with a possibly unreliable narrator/consciousness in Tom. The play with point of view is important to the questions the story raises about ethics (human beings are making a planet habitable to themselves by exterminating the dominant native species), about how we view ethical problems (Tom's Amerindian heritage marks him as a member of a race nearly exterminated by white settlers), and about the far reaching effects of human decisions (in spite of the passage of time, Tom still carries with him both the victim's sense of alienation and, because of his mixed heritage, the white man's burden of guilt). Thus the manipulations of point of view help the writer present a set of important cultural and racial issues in intensely personal terms that do justice to the complexity of the issues.

Such mixing of points of view has, of course, its dangers for both writer and reader. The unskillful writer may shift carelessly or illogically or may signal those shifts inadequately and lose the reader. The unskilled reader may fail to notice the verbal or graphic signals of shifts and may thus lose the way himself. Despite such dangers, point of view remains an area of technique that continues to attract variation and experimentation, for it also remains a key means by which to explore the problems of how our perceptions of reality are shaped or limited by our senses, our personalities, and our particular social, racial and historical contexts.

LANGUAGE

Sounds, Words and Sentences

In all forms of communication—writing, speaking, film, television—there is a crucial relationship between *what* is being said and the *way* in which it is being presented. For example, whether a person chooses to express his views about a particular issue via a cartoon or a written editorial will influence his message and how his audience reacts to it. Even though the relationship between a message and how it is presented seems obvious, the concept presents difficulty because a distinction is sometimes made (especially in literature) between "form" and "content." There is an assumption being made that it is somehow possible to separate a writer's "style" from the "content" of his work: two or more writers may deal with the theme of alienation from society (content) but their writing styles (form) will differ. Perhaps it is easiest to solve this problem by dispensing with the word "content" and by using the word "information" instead. Examine these three sentences:

> The storm ruined his crops.
> His crops were ruined by the storm.
> What ruined his crops was the storm.

The information being conveyed by all the sentences is the same: He had some crops and the storm destroyed them. But is the meaning or content in all three sentences exactly the same? In the first of the three sentences, the emphasis seems to be on the storm. Perhaps this sentence might appear in an episode about a terrible storm which, among other things, destroyed his crops. In the second sentence, the emphasis is on the crops—the storm may not be all that significant. In the third sentence, the emphasis is on the ruination or destruction of the crops. A careful author will in all forms of writing consciously manipulate his choice of words and how he puts them together because these variations will allow him to control what he communicates to his readers.

Sounds

In spoken language sounds play a vital role. Whether a message is a scream of pain, a shout of joy, a snicker, a grunt, or a complex combination of sequenced sounds (as in words and sentences), the message is carried by those sounds. In written English the sounds are roughly represented by a set of symbols—a,b,c,d, etc.— which are combined to form words on a page. Writers often take advantage of how words sound to make whatever they are describing more vivid and more real. In Harlan Ellison's story " 'Repent, Harlequin!' Said the Ticktockman" when fifty thousand dollars worth of jelly beans roll down the expresstrip it is easy to see and hear them "bouncing jouncing tumbling clittering clattering skittering" because of Ellison's choice of words. He uses words that *sound* like what they mean (clittering, clattering, skittering). He also dramatizes the visual effect of millions of jelly beans by rhyming words (bouncing, jouncing) and by stringing them together without commas so that the reader will read them all at once without stopping.

Two very common techniques which can be used to help convey or intensify meaning are *alliteration* and *rhythm*. Alliteration is the repetition of initial consonant sounds. Advertisers use it all the time: Better Buy Bodkin Bananas. Alliteration can be used to help a reader visualize an eerie forest floor like the one described in H.P. Lovecraft's"Colour Out of Space": "too soft with dank moss and matting of infinite years of decay." Notice how the alliterative effect is created not only by the repetition of the initial sounds (*m*oss, *m*atting, *d*ank, *d*ecay), but also by the repetition of other sounds as well: s*o*ft, m*o*ss, d*a*nk, m*a*tting, dan*k*, de*c*ay. Alliteration is often used to create a marching tempo: "And so it goes. And so it goes. And so it

69

goes. And so it goes goes goes goes goes tick tock tick tock tick tock" which tells the reader exactly how it feels to be in a society where every little bit of business is rigorously regulated ("Repent, Harlequin"). As in the above example, alliteration is also often used to create rhythm, which is nothing more than an effect produced by a repetition of sound or motion at regular intervals. Rhythm can be produced by repeating a sound, a word, a group of words, or a sentence. H.P. Lovecraft in "The Colour Out of Space" uses rhythm to help the reader visualize the small farms which dot the countryside: "...there were little hillside farms; *sometimes* with all the buildings standing, *sometimes* with only one or two, and *sometimes* with only a lonely chimney or a fast-filling cellar" (our italics).

In English, there are rules which govern the combination of sounds. Some sounds can be put together: *shrine, brine, twine;* others cannot: *lknine, bquine, fgine.* Although writers usually don't violate these combining rules, they can do so. In his Cthulhu stories, Lovecraft emphasizes the strangeness and mystery of his alien creatures and the rituals associated with them by devising chants such as "Ph'nglui mglw'hafh Cthulju R'lyeh wgah'nagl fhtagn." Sometimes a science fiction writer might want to call a small furry alien a "dleen"; or an alien character might have a name such as Gj'Bpotik. Combining the sounds in ways which are not found in English emphasizes the alienness of the species or character.

Words

Sounds are an important part of writing. But the writer also controls his message to the reader by a careful selection of the words he uses. Precise word choice and modification enable a writer to breathe life into his stories. Consider this sentence from J.G. Ballard's "Subliminal Man":

Sirens blaring, two patrol cars swung up on to the verge through
the crowd and plunged across the damp grass.

✓ Notice how the action becomes more vivid, the picture
more real through Ballard's choice of words. He tells
exactly how many cars there were, what kind of cars they
were, and how they were driven. He even describes the
condition of the grass.

To further illustrate this point, let us examine this
excerpt from "The Veldt" by Ray Bradbury:

... you could feel the prickling fur on your hand, and your mouth
was stuffed with the dusty upholstery smell of their heated pelts,
and the yellow of them was in your eyes like the yellow of an
exquisite French tapestry, the yellows of lions and summer
grass, and the sound of the matted lion lungs exhaling on the
silent noontide, and the smell of meat from the panting, dripping
mouths.

The information conveyed in this passage could have
been recorded in a sentence such as: "the lions were
standing in the grass, nearby." But Bradbury creates a
fuller experience for the reader by carefully selecting his
words.

But careful selection is not simply a matter of
supplying more words; rather it means the choice of the
specific words which best express the precise shade of
meaning the writer wants to convey. In addition to their
"dictionary meaning," most words have associations
which affect people. Compare the feelings associated with
the word "lady" to those associated with the word
"chick." Or compare the feelings associated with the word
"home" to those associated with "shack." Or "thin,"
"slender," "skinny,""scrawny." A pleasant easy-going
person might be seen as being slender. A tiresome,
annoying person often is perceived as being skinny or
scrawny. Isaac Asimov foreshadows the madness and
destruction of the approaching "Nightfall" with his
description of the red sun Beta's rays: They cast a "square

of *bloody* sunlight." "Bloody" suggests not only the color red, but violent destruction, impending doom.

Words not only paint pictures or evoke feelings, they can also control the distance between a writer and his audience. The selection of pronouns in a piece of writing can create a sense of immediacy between the author and the reader or it can remove them from each other. First person narratives usually employ the pronoun "I" and create a personal bond between the narrator and the reader. The distance between a writer or narrator and his audience is also influenced by the kinds of words used in a piece. The narrator in "The Colour Out of Space" speaks in the first person (I), but he never seems very close to the reader—there is distance. Perhaps this distance is, in part, created by the words Lovecraft has the narrator use: "Only with persistent knocking could I rouse the aged man, and when he shuffled timidly to the door I could tell he was not glad to see me" rather than "Only with repeating banging could I wake the old guy, and when he came shyly to the door I could see he wasn't happy to see me."

This matter of selecting "aged" rather than "old" or "man" rather than "guy" is usually referred to as "level of formality." Certainly "guy" is less formal than "man," which is less formal than "gentleman." Compare the narrator's choice of words in Lovecraft's "The Colour Out of Space" ("furtive, chiaroscuro, desolation, miasmal, malleable") to the Harlequin's choice of words in Ellison's "Repent, Harlequin" ("fight, dumb, get stuffed, you're full of it, hate, lie, idiot"). The words the Harlequin uses tell the reader something about his character: he is probably young, brash, impatient, and not too impressed with status and societal rules and regulations. By contrast, the narrator of "The Colour Out of Space" seems to be a genteel, well-educated, *reserved* individual, and the horrors of the alien infestation that he describes appear both more frightening and more credible because he is probably exercising great restraint in relating his story.

Thus, the formality of words is important in creating characters and narrators.

Up to this point words have been examined in isolation. But another important aspect of word selection is how words act together with other words. Generally speaking, combinations like "ridiculous tree" don't make much sense. The meaning of "tree" and the meaning of "ridiculous" seem to exclude one another. However, these word combination constraints are often violated in literature. A poet writing about the futility of technology might want to speak of "an abominable elevator." Or a science fiction writer might combine words differently to show that a culture has an advanced technology. In "Repent, Harlequin" workers release their "a-grav plates." Ellison even combines and modifies words to form new words such as "wegglers" or "swizzleskid."

Sentences

Again, meaning isn't just words, it's how words are put together with other words:

> John hit Mary.
> Mary hit John.

The words are exactly the same and of course the sentences mean very different things. Sounds and words provide many options for a writer; sentences, too, offer infinite variety. Sentences can be very long and complicated, forcing the reader to concentrate on each and every word, every nuance of meaning. Or they can be short. A sentence can be arranged so that its meaning, for the sake of creating suspense or curiosity is until the very end, incomplete. Harlan Ellison in "Repent Harlequin" varies the length and complexity of his sentences all through the story.

Although different sentence variations can be used to convey the same information, the variations provide the capability to emphasize one element over another or to delete information entirely. Examine this sentence from Lovecraft's "The Colour Out of Space": "Twilight had now fallen, and lanterns were brought from the house." Lovecraft's narrator could have conveyed the same information: "Twilight had now fallen, and from the house the men brought lanterns." Instead he chose to emphasize *lanterns* rather than who was bringing them (the men) or from where they were brought (from the house). In fact, *who* brought the lanterns is so unimportant at this point in the narration that the information is deleted entirely: "Twilight had now fallen and the lanterns were brought from the house" (by the men).

Generally, the rules which govern how words are put together to form sentences are not violated in prose fiction. Even poetry, where these violations occur more frequently (such as in e.e. cummings', "pity this busy monster, manunkind, /not"), most often preserves sentence structure. Here is an example:

> I had a dream, which was not at all a dream.
> The bright sun was extinguished, and the stars
> Did wander darkling in the eternal space,
> Rayless and pathless, and the icy Earth
> Swung blind and blackening in the moonless air.
> ("Darkness," George Gordon, Lord Byron)

Sometimes, though, violations of rules which govern sentence formation are found in prose. In "Gone Are the Lupo," by James Hickey, the inability of Man and Moomie to communicate is seen in the contrasting language:

> "I am dance the dance of night and new Master and old Master say oh ho ho ho ho and are go first this way and that way and shake many way. Many moisture are run from eyes."

> "Oh no," say one new Master and roll on floor. "Oh
> youre killing me. Make it stop, Jack!"

These syntactic violations suggest an alien species whose
minds exhibit thought patterns quite different from our
own.

Science Fiction as a genre often explores alien
cultures, whether the alienness derives from other kinds
of beings or only from ourselves in different times, places,
or states of consciousness. It is a unique challenge to the
writer to create alien characters, settings, or cultures that
seem real; after all, they are not a part of the reader's
immediate, everyday experience. Language is a powerful
tool that can be used in a variety of ways to emphasize the
alienness of a character, culture, or future time.

Imagery and Figurative Language

We know that words carry information, and we have
seen that words have affective functions, too. Often, the
way words affect us is quite different from what the literal
meanings of the words would lead someone unfamiliar
with our language to believe. When a speaker says "I'm
dead tired," or "It's as hot as hell outside," the messages
received are not literal interpretations: the speaker is
exhausted, but certainly not approaching death, and
while it may be uncomfortably warm outside, the speaker
has neither melted nor suffered the agonies of Dante's
Inferno. The assumptions we make when we use such
figures of speech are part of the process by which we
communicate as speakers of the same language.

Unfortunately, imagery and figurative language
frequently are misunderstood to be only decorations
found in poetry: pretty, but not too functional, and
certainly not important to an understanding of language
or literature. Just the opposite is true. We delight in
friends who can, with a few descriptive or comparative
phrases, make us see persons, places, and events as they
did. Some such phrases have even been employed until

they have become *cliches*, expressions used so often that their freshness has worn off and we are hardly aware that they are figures of speech: "dead tired," "red as a rose," "hard as nails," pretty as a picture," and "sweet as sugar" are cliches. Undoubtedly, there was a time when "hot as hell" conjured up horrifying visions of fiery torment in the minds of readers or listeners, that is, a time when to say that something was "hell" was actually to help describe it. And that is the purpose of imagery and figurative language: to aid the reader or listener in feeling, as well as intellectually understanding, what is being presented by making concrete and vivid what might otherwise be vague.

Imagery

One way statements can be made vivid is through the representation of sensory experience in words, through appeals to our awareness of sight, smell, taste, hearing, or touch; this representation is called *imagery*. When an author writes that a hillside is "smooth," a waterfall is "green," or an unknown liquid is "sour" and "bubbly," the author is providing familiar sensory clues to enable the reader more readily to perceive what may be unfamiliar. In "The Veldt," Ray Bradbury wanted his readers to share two parents' fears about their nursery, a specially designed room which transforms the children's thoughts into three-dimensional images. The same passage we quoted earlier in this chapter takes on new dimensions when we recognize that the principle behind Bradbury's selection of words was to provide vivid sensory detail to help the reader feel what the parents felt.

And here were the lions now, fifteen feet away, so real, so feverishly and startlingly real that you could feel the prickling fur on your hand, and your mouth was stuffed with the dusty upholstery smell of their heated pelts, and the yellow of them was in your eyes like the yellow of an exquisite French tapestry, the yellow of lions and summer grass, and the sound of the matted lion lungs exhaling on the silent noontide, and the smell of meat from the panting, dripping mouths.

If Bradbury had written that the room was "frightening," instead of using imagery, the nursery would not have been felt to be nearly so much of a threat.

Imagery is especially important when an author is trying to create an alien world: the unknown can only be understood in the terminology of the known. For example, when Clifford D. Simak, in "Desertion," wanted to explain the beauty of Jupiter as seen by the men who took on Jovian lifeforms, he wrote of a "drifting purple mist that moved like fleeing shadows over a red and purple sward" and of music "like bells might make from some steeple on a sunny, springtime hill." To say that an alien world is "unimaginable" or "unbelievable" may create a sense of wonder, but it cannot create a sense of participation in the way that imagery involving what is already familiar to the reader can.

Occasionally, an author who wants to create an air of unreality uses *synesthesia,* a mingling of sensory experiences. As Tom Two Ribbons joins a group of aliens in a ritual communion in "Sundance," Silverberg uses synesthesia to illustrate the way Tom's perceptions have been distorted by the oxygen he has sniffed: "The scent of their bodies is fiery red to me. Their soft cries are puffs of steam." The reader tries to comprehend Tom's experience and, because we normally do not smell colors or see sounds, determines that Tom's mind is disordered.

Figurative Language

Imagery is often used in conjunction with *figurative language,* words and expressions used out of their literal context. Several forms of figurative language—*metaphor, implied metaphor, personification,* and *simile*—are based on analogy, or comparison.

A *metaphor* is a comparison which identifies one thing with another thing which is basically unlike it. If someone were being particularly stubborn, our first reaction might be to say, "He is a mule." Despite our knowledge that man and mule are not literally the same, we feel that an identification exists. This is how metaphors are made. A statue does not move; and people can hold themselves nearly immobile; therefore, "Braxa was a statue, both hands raised to her face, elbows high and outspread" (Roger Zelazny, "A Rose for Ecclesiastes"). This process yields metaphors such as the "sky was an unclouded pool of turquoise" and the "desert was a carpet of endless orange" ("A Rose for Ecclesiastes"). The sentence "A book is an object," however, does not contain a metaphor, because a book clearly *is* an object. The things being compared must differ in kind. And such comparisons aren't merely decorations. They are evaluations, recognitions of similarity that enable a reader more easily to understand whatever is being presented.

Metaphors may be *implied* as well as stated. Thus, there is an implicit comparison between administration and puppetry when an official is asked to "pull a few strings." Harlan Ellison makes a similar analogy between the bureaucracy of a future society and a web in " 'Repent, Harlequin!' Said the Ticktockman": "the Ticktockman managed to pull the proper threads of government webbing...." In the same way, Herman Melville could write: "The far summit fairly smoked with frost..." ("The Tartarus of Maids"). The comparison is not directly stated as "The summit was a chimney," but the analogy is plain nonetheless.

Personification is a type of metaphor in which a comparison is made between the animate and the inanimate, giving something inanimate the characteristics of life. With personification, the heath could "slumber," shadows could "lurk," and the wind might have "shrieked and howled" (H.P. Lovecraft, "The

Colour Out of Space"). Personification is the basis of Robert Sheckly's "Specialist," in which the engine, walls and accumulators of a spaceship have actually become characters. This movement from the figurative to the literal is more common in science fiction than in other types of literature and is a way to utilize personification as foreshadowing or for dramatic effect. If a character thinks that the plants in a forest are watching him or whispering about his movements, they may in fact *be* sentient creatures with power to help or harm him. What appeared to be personification may prove to be literally true, and the reader has been given a clue, but a clue he was expected to misinterpret; thus, when the reader learns the truth, he is more strongly affected than if he had only been told "On Eutiptkon, plants are conscious creatures."

It is obvious that no two different things being compared are exactly alike. "He is a mule," makes such an identification. If, however, we were to say "He is like a mule," or "He is as stubborn as a mule," instead of "He is a mule," we would have pointed up our awareness that while some similarities exist between man and mule, the two are not identical. The use of such phraseology, with "like" or "as," is called a *simile*. A simile is not as direct a comparison as a metaphor; it appears more objective, but the descriptive element is not lost. In "A Rose for Ecclesiastes," Roger Zelazny uses similes to make a Martian matriarch and a Martian instrument seem almost familiar: "With her rainbow of voluminous skirts she looked like an inverted punch bowl set atop a cushion"; "The stringed-thing throbbed like a toothache, and a tick-tocking, like ghosts of all the clocks they had never invented, sprang from the block."

Allusion and Verbal Irony[1]

Allusion, reference to a person, place, event, object, or

---

[1]Other types of irony are discussed in the chapter "Tone."

process, is also an affective device. When Harlan Ellison writes that the Harlequin was "a Bolivar; a Napoleon; a Robin Hood; a Dick Bong (Ace of Aces); a Jesus; a Jomo Kenyatta" (" 'Repent, Harlequin!' Said the Tick-tockman"), he is evoking the reader's feelings about these figures from history, legend and popular culture, and applying these feelings to the Harlequin. Allusion, then, is a shortcut to emotional response. The references may be religious: "This is the body, this is the blood, take, eat, join" (Robert Silverberg, "Sundance") can arouse the deep emotions associated with the Christian ritual of communion; and "The Book of Revelations" in Isaac Asimov's "Nightfall" is an allusion both to that book of the New Testament, otherwise known as "The Apocalypse," and to the Bible as a whole. Or they may be classical: the allusion to Tartarus, the lowest reach of Hell to which Zeus assigned the defeated Titans, quickly indicates that Herman Melville sees the paper-mill as a modern form of Hell in "The Tartarus of Maids." Allusions may be literary, historical, logical, astrological, contemporary, ancient and, especially in science fiction, scientific. The reference to the discovery of the law of gravitation in Asimov's "Nightfall" is an allusion to the discovery on earth and suggests that aspects of the real and fictional worlds may be analogous. Indeed, sometimes allusions have multiple associations. In "The Machine Stops," by E.M. Forster, Kuno asks his mother if she knows "four big stars that form an oblong and three stars close together in the middle of that oblong and hanging from these stars, three other stars." He is describing what we know as the constellation Orion, an astronomical allusion which has astrological and mythological dimensions as well.

Since allusion is based on previous reader knowledge, the reader must be acquainted with what is being alluded to for the allusion to function. A foreigner might need to have an allusion to Shakespeare or to John F. Kennedy explained, and "in jokes" are usually confusing to those who are not members of the group. The more we know, the more we can find in what we read. In some cases, recognition of the allusion is necessary for the reader to understand the meaning of the story: the reader who is unfamiliar with the myth of the Minotaur misses the point of Jorge Luis Borges' "The House of Asterion," in which the Minotaur, usually a monster, arouses our sympathy with his monologue, his identity unclear until his slayer, usually portrayed as the hero, reveals it at the end of the story. On the other hand, most allusions are relatively easy to locate. Most of those mentioned above can be found in a college dictionary, and one can find out more about Orion and the Minotaur in a handbook of mythology. The constellation Orion can be identified from a simple star chart. The more we read, however, the more we are afforded the pleasure of recognizing such allusions on our own. Properly used, allusions are intended not to puzzle us or to impress us with the author's erudition, but to suggest significant connections and associations between the contexts in which they occur and the context of our culture as a whole.

A subtle and sometimes complex device which also relies on the reader's knowledge and perception is *verbal irony,* in which what is said is *not* what is meant. What is meant may in fact be the opposite of what is said. In " 'Repent, Harlequin!' Said the Ticktockman," by Harlan Ellison, a character's notice of "termination," a mandate from the government indicating that his life is to end, is described as a "billet-doux," or love note: it brings a message of death, however, rather than one of love. Or the irony might be in the use of a deliberate understatement. When in Roger Zelazny's "A Rose for Ecclesiastes," Gallinger is awakened in the middle of the night, he queries "...isn't the hour a trifle awkward?": he means, of course, that the hour is very awkward. An author may make a statement and then undercut it in order to show his ironic intent. In "The Subliminal Man," J.G. Ballard writes: "Whatever other criticisms might be levelled at the present society, it certainly knew how to build roads." Then he spends two paragraphs describing the clutter of freeways, the congestion they have caused, and the additional miles and time they require. His meaning is clear: the society, despite appearances, does not construct roads any more reasonably than it does anything else. He blames by seeming to praise.

Allusions and irony do require a sophistication on the part of the reader, and the ability to deal with both is a mark of the educated person. It is not simply a matter of social refinement, as some utilitarians would suggest, but a matter of efficient and effective communication, using the language and culture which are ours.

TONE

One way an author expresses meaning is through *tone,* which may be defined as the writer's attitude toward his or her characters and subject as expressed by word choice and rhythm. We are all familiar with how tone works in our daily speech; we may, for example, say "thank you" in ways which can express anything from enthusiastic appreciation to noncommittal gratitude to the exact opposite of appreciation. Without our being overly subtle, the listener will get the message. In literature, on the other hand, especially in that which is meant to be read, the author does not have the advantage of being able to speak to us; he or she must convey attitude by means limited to the way words are put on a page. This is not entirely a handicap, since the written language is a remarkably versatile tool; however, sensitivity to the nuances of tone requires a certain amount of alertness in the reader that may not always be needed when listening to the spoken word.

For example, take an opening paragraph of the story " 'Repent, Harlequin!' Said the Ticktockman":

But because it was the very world it was, the very world they had allowed it to *become,* for months his activities did not come to the alarmed attention of The Ones Who Kept The Machines Functioning Smoothly, the ones who poured the very best butter over the cams and mainsprings of culture. Not until it had become obvious that somehow, someway, he had become a notoriety, a celebrity, perhaps even a hero for (what Officialdom inescapably tagged) "an emotionally disturbed segment of the populace," did they turn it over to the Ticktockman and his legal machinery.

Even if we have never read this story before, we will probably recognize what Ellison's attitude really is here and whose side he is on. By repeating the word "world" and by italicizing "become" (emphasizing it in the way a stress in speech emphasizes it), he indicates that something is wrong with the society he has set up. By referring to rulers of the society with words which have come to bear negative connotations and, more importantly, by capitalizing those words so as to undercut any positive value they may have, Ellison clues us in on who the enemy is. Furthermore, in describing the central opponent of authority (Harlequin) in words which move from negative to positive in connotative value (notoriety, celebrity, hero), we get the feeling that Ellison is preparing to introduce us to a hero, one who is going to rebel against the rigid, clockwork society indicated in this passage. Finally, by calling the embodiment of authority the "Ticktockman"—the name the story's public gives him when his back is turned—the author emphasizes the man's impersonal rigidity and prevents us from feeling either sympathy or awe for him; he effectively dehumanizes him for us. It is as if the Ticktockman had the face of a clock.

Rhythm and word choice also contribute to the *mood* of a piece of literature, another aspect of tone. The mood is in the "feeling" of the piece; in the passage above, the italicized word, the capitalized words, and the jumble of phrases of varied length describing both Harlequin and the authorities help create a playful anarchic mood which suits the actions of the hero and which is completely antagonistic to the clockwork mechanism of the society and the minds of its rulers. Mood can be better understood by thinking of it as the background music of a story, because like the music of a television show or a movie it focuses our feelings about the characters and subjects of a work.

Suppose Ellison were in complete sympathy with the authority of the society in his story. One way the passage discussed above might read is this:

> Because of the lack of complete vigilance in this society, perhaps due to a certain permissiveness inherent in all reasonable social structures, the activities of this individual did not come to the attention of the authorities for several months. At first officials were reluctant to apprehend someone who seemed merely to be a harmless eccentric; but it became increasingly clear that his not-so-harmless antics were infecting an emotionally disturbed segment of the populace. It was at this point, and only at this point, that the Master Timekeeper was called in.

We recognize in this passage an increased formality in the words chosen. Furthermore, while in the previous passage the words used to describe officialdom and its works were capitalized so as to ridicule what they described, in this passage those words are treated with respect. Phrases such as "due to a certain permissiveness inherent in all reasonable social structures" and "only at this point" tend to justify authority as something essentially benevolent but driven to harsh measures by this threat to society. The Ticktockman is called the "Master Timekeeper," which is his official title in the story. There is also a curious neutrality about the person in question. He is referred to as "this individual" and a "harmless eccentric" who performs "not so harmless antics" which "infect" the populace—the writer could just as well be describing a microbe. The rhythm is less sprightly than that of the first passage; there are no italics or eccentrically capitalized words, and the phrases and clauses are longer and less varied in length. It is smoother, more orderly, and the speaker's voice takes itself more seriously, as it should: it is, after all, the voice of power—controlled, reasonable, but rightly upset by the threat of disorder.

Of course, tone may express more than a hostile or sympathetic attitude, or create a grim or playful mood. A work such as Pohl's "Day Million" has a narrator who is condescending to his audience and at the same time enthusiastic about the subject he is talking about—a love affair of the future. Whether or not this is Pohl's real attitude is for the reader to decide, but "Day Million" shows that a writer can create tones of complexity which do not always lead us by the nose to his or her "real" feelings about something. An example of a different kind of tone is the quiet that surrounds the action, description, and dialogue of Theodore Sturgeon's "Slow Sculpture":

> He looked at a compact girl in her mid-twenties, at a fearless face and eyes the same color as her hair, which was extraordinary because her hair was red-gold. She looked down at a leather-skinned man in his forties, at a gold-leaf electroscope in his hand, and felt she was an intruder.
> She said, "Oh–" in what was apparently the right way.
> Because he nodded once and said, "Hold this–" and there could be no thought of intrusion.

Like other varieties of tone, this one is again created chiefly by rhythm and word choice. The rhythm is controlled by the use of short paragraphs, sometimes only a sentence or two in length, and very sparse dialogue. The kind of word choice here helps to create the story's mood of quiet intimacy, which is of course appropriate for a love story. The man and woman are referred to only as "he" and "she" throughout the story. Their surroundings are hardly described at all, which gives the reader the feeling that these two people are the only ones who exist in the universe.

The varieties of tone a writer can create are many. One of the most important varieties, however, is irony.

Irony

Irony is a term with many meanings, all of which are associated with contrast or incongruity. One form of irony, verbal irony, in which what is said is contrasted with what is meant, was discussed in the chapter on language. Three other forms—dramatic irony, irony of situation, and irony of structure—are also important literary techniques. With them an author may indirectly evaluate, sometimes even mock, a character, an institution, or a set of values; he may provide changes in perspective which lead us to make re-evaluations; and he may reveal some of the complexities of human impulses, actions and responses.

Dramatic irony involves a contrast between what a character says and what the reader knows is true. An author thus is enabled to suggest an evaluation of the speaker without directly telling us what to think of his or her character. In D.M. Thomas's "Tithonus," after we have read of Edgar L. Cummings, a man whose brain alone is being kept artificially functional long after the "death" of the rest of his body, and after we have seen him treated as a laboratory curiosity while his deepest emotions are evoked on cue for visitors, the speaker, a guide, says: "I hope and believe he'd thank us.../ if he could,/ And say moreover how proud he is being/ our proto-immortal...." We know there is little in Edgar L. Cummings's situation for which to be thankful; but the speaker does not see any of the human pain we do: to him, Cummings is only an interesting specimen. The speaker's disregard for what we have come to believe is important reveals to us his insensitivity and supplies a comment on the danger of a facile faith in science exercised without real human concern. Another example occurs in E.M. Forster's "The Machine Stops" when Vashti, an intellectual who has lived in an underground world in which art and music are transmitted electronically, first travels to see her son. She surveys the mountains of Asia and the islands of Greece which have inspired poets and philosophers for centuries, only to comment: "No ideas here." We see, as Vashti does not, that despite her interest in ideas, she is too isolated by her belief in the enclosed world of the Machine to ever have any new ideas.

Her underground society can only regress, not progress.

In *irony of situation,* the contrast is between what is expected by the characters involved in the situation and what actually occurs, or between what would seem suitable in a given situation and what actually is. Thus, it is ironic in Shelley's "Ozymandias" that the fragments of a statue of a king who proclaimed his empire's greatness lie half-buried in the desolation of a desert. He had expected his renown to continue unabated. The irony of the situation brings us directly to the theme, the transitory nature of earthly glory. In " 'Repent, Harlequin!' Said the Ticktockman," it is ironic that the Master Timekeeper, the powerful symbol of absolute accuracy and control who has men killed for any failure to maintain the time schedule, is himself late at the end of the story and unable to face the evidence of his human fallibility. He had hardly expected himself to be unable to meet the schedule. And it is ironic in Bradbury's "The Veldt" that the two-dimensional, telepathic nursery which George and Lydia bought because "nothing's too good for our children" leads them to abdicate their responsibilities as parents and cause their own destruction. The children use the nursery to kill their parents. It would seem appropriate that a scientifically-designed psychological tool like the nursery should fulfill its function of reducing childhood neuroses: instead, the nursery is overused and increases the neuroses it is expected to relieve; it allows the children to revel in the expression of the more violent aspects of their minds. Bradbury uses irony to establish what he believes the relationship between parent and child should be and to indicate his disapproval of a society in which human responsibility is delegated to a machine.

In *irony of structure,* the contrast is between what we as readers expect to happen in a work of literature and what actually happens. A twist causes us to re-examine our assumptions about what has gone before: the ironic trick is played on the reader instead of on a character. One of the best examples of irony of structure is Borges's "House of Asterion." Borges takes us through paragraph after paragraph with the narrator, and we sympathize with him, feel for his loneliness. We learn that he has killed, but he has killed with the belief that men have come to him to be delivered from the world's evil. Only in the last line, when Theseus says, "The Minotaur scarcely defended himself," do we discover that the narrator was the Minotaur, the hated monster. Borges has guided us, but without forcing us by stating the issues directly, to ask ourselves what "monster" really means and to consider the complexities of personal interaction when there is so much we do not understand about ourselves and others.

This, then, is the value of irony: its indirection. Meaning is clear without being stated. The contrasts are set up for us, but we make the discoveries ourselves. Forster does not have to tell us that Vashti is blind to the outside world around her, nor does Thomas have to tell us that the narrator of "Tithonus" is not a trustworthy source of values: we know, because we have seen the connections between the contrasts the authors provided, and we are the more convinced because we were shown, not told. We saw the relationships for ourselves.

Since we are led to understand something which is not stated directly, irony usually is considered one of the most sophisticated of the literary techniques. Irony may be quite complex: an author may use several forms in a single work, and the forms may be mingled subtly together. "Tithonus," for example, involves not only dramatic irony, but also irony of situation: Cummings's position is not the one he would have expected, nor is it appropriate. Irony is a challenge: its effectiveness rests in our ability to use our intelligence to understand what the author meant by what he or she did not say.

THEME AND VALUE

Theme

Perhaps the most basic descriptive statement we can make with reference to a piece of literature is that it is about something. Ellison's " 'Repent, Harlequin!' Said the Ticktockman" is about a man who rebels against a repressive society of the future. Clarke's "The Sentinel" is about the discovery of an alien device on the moon. Archibald MacLeish's poem "The End of the World" is about how the world ends. Some works tell us about things that are very familiar to us; others tell us about specialized, unique events that we are not very likely to experience. For example, Asimov's "Nightfall" describes how the people of a particular planet react to a natural disaster—a total eclipse. Whether a story, poem, or play is about something familiar or unfamiliar, each one tells of something unique and particular; no two poems about love are exactly alike; no two space adventures have the same hero fighting the same alien under exactly the same circumstances.

Although every piece of literature is about something particular, some works, in addition, seem to make statements about very broad concerns. To illustrate this idea, let us imagine a story about a young man's painful first experience with love. It is possible that the story, while relating a specific set of incidents, might also be saying something about the process of growing up and how this process inevitably causes a loss of innocence. Thus, the writer has used a story about young love as a vehicle or means of making some observations or sharing his insights about an inevitable part of living—growth and maturation. This element of the story which goes outside of the story, which goes beyond the particular that the story is about, is called the *theme*. Then, the story is about a young man's first unsuccessful love experience, and the theme of the story might be that falling in love, an inevitable process of growth, can cause us to lose some of our innocence. You've probably heard the saying "sadder but wiser." For another example, the title of "The End of the World" tells us what the poem is about; but MacLeish chooses a circus as the setting in which we witness that end, and he describes that moment when "the top blew off" as revealing "There in the sudden blackness the black pall/ Of nothing, nothing, nothing—nothing at all." Thus he makes the thematic statement that the absurdity of the world is a symptom of the fact that nothingness underlies all existence.

Not every story has a theme, but it is entirely possible for some stories to have more than one theme, and this thematic multiplicity often enriches a work. Our story about a young man's first experience with love might have additional themes: perhaps the author wishes to make observations not only about the loss of innocence but about the nature of love as well. Of course, it is not always easy to be absolutely sure about what a piece of literature has to say. We have to be careful not to "read into" a story a meaning that actually isn't there. Every story about a young man's first love doesn't necessarily have a theme concerning the loss of innocence. In fact, stories which are about entirely different things often share similar themes. So, a story about a man who robs a grocery store could have the loss of innocence as one of its themes.

In science fiction, stories are often grouped thematically. That is, if you read a collection of science fiction, you might see that the table of contents is divided into sections with titles such as "The Threat of Technology." Such a section could include diverse stories like Ellison's " 'Repent, Harlequin!' Said the

Ticktockman," Ballard's "The Subliminal Man," and Forster's "The Machine Stops." Each story tells about a different thing, yet a theme which they all share is that technology can be a greater danger to a society if people ultimately become ruled by the very machines which were created to serve them.

We have already said that one of the difficulties with the concept of theme is that it is not always obvious what the theme of a work of literature is, and we don't want to make any observations about a work unless they are justified by elements in the piece. Certainly an author wants the readers to see any themes that are there, but a careful writer often wants his readers to feel that they have discovered what he is saying. Nobody likes to be preached at, and we are less likely to take a pronouncement seriously if it is forced upon us, than if we must read a piece of literature carefully and think about it in order to understand what is being said.

There is no simple formula or procedure which will enable a reader to discover the theme or themes of a literary work. But theme is always presented by a manipulation of such elements as characterization, plot, setting, point of view, language or tone. Let us examine a few stories and see how the authors have controlled various elements within these stories in order to present their themes.

As we have already mentioned, "Nightfall," by Asimov is about how the populace of a particular planet react in the face of a catastrophe—a total eclipse. Of course, on the planet Earth a total eclipse of the sun has never caused absolute destruction even when the phenomenon was not understood, because, having only one sun, we are familiar with darkness, and the whole thing doesn't last very long. Asimov presents us with a situation, however, where a planet, Lagash, has six suns, at least one of which is *always* in the sky. Hence the populace never experiences total darkness except once every two thousand and fifty years when the single remaining sun on one side of the planet is eclipsed for a whole day. Presumably the people, unable to cope with darkness and stars since they are entirely out of the realm of their experience, go mad every two thousand and fifty years and destroy whatever civilization has been established up to that point. Lagash is literally caught in a vicious cycle and never can progress beyond the level that has been reached immediately before the eclipse.

What can the theme of such a story be? What do these events on Lagash have to do with us here on Earth? In order to answer these questions we must go beyond what the story is "about." First, let's look at the plot. There seems to be a conflict between two groups in the story: the scientists and the Cultists. The scientists have examined the data which they've collected and the laws which they've formulated and want to explain the approaching darkness as an eclipse, a natural phenomenon which can be dealt with by retreating to artificially lighted rooms for the duration of the darkness. The Cultists, however, refuse to question the *Book of Revelations,* which explains the darkness in another way. To them the alternate explanation and preparation for the eclipse devised by the scientists is blasphemous. We, as readers, are given the opportunity to see that the scientists are "right" because the eclipse does occur at the end of the story, and the darkness does cause madness. The scientists offer the only way for the planet Lagash to escape from its vicious cycle.

If we examine the characterization within the story, we are given more clues as to its meaning. The scientists are presented as rational beings who are willing to examine data and retain or discard various explanations of natural phenomena on the basis of those data. The Cultists are presented as fanatics who refuse to be swayed by even the strongest evidence. In fact, by inciting a riot they attempt to destroy the observatory where the scientists are preparing for the disaster. At this point, we should begin to realize that Asimov is "stacking the deck" against the Cultists; we can also observe that throughout the story the scientists seem to be associated with light and the Cultists with darkness. It is quite safe to say, then, that one of the themes of this story is: Science can make human progress possible, while superstition and religious dogma often hinder it. Asimov could have written a story about the same planet with the problem of an approaching eclipse and have manipulated the plot, characters and other elements to produce an entirely different theme. His scientists could have been presented as fanatics who successfully seize control of the government and force the populace to be confined to lighted rooms during the eclipse. Then the civilization could continue to develop, new technology could be achieved, and the planet Lagash could have an atomic war which destroys the entire population; no one would be around for the next eclipse. This would certainly be a different statement about what science has to offer!

The story "Nightfall" is a good example of how plot and characterization can play vital roles in revealing the theme. Other elements such as setting are also important, but in a story such as "The Machine Stops," setting plays an even more active part in revealing theme. The setting, in effect, becomes the hero's major antagonist. The machine has become the total environment and in so doing it has made the society completely dependent upon it and has deprived the humans of their individuality. These implications of the setting are revealed by language as well. The initial setting is described with a simile as "a small room hexagonal in shape, like the cell of a bee," a comparison which associates the extreme order of a hive with the machine environment.

In another story, Pohl's "Day Million," characterization, plot and setting are not nearly as important for revealing the theme of the story as language, tone and point of view. "Day Million" is about how two people of the future, Dora and Don, fall in love. But the plot, which could have given us a detailed description of how Don and Dora met, exactly what they said to each other, and how their love developed, doesn't do so. The characters of Dora and Don aren't developed, either. What is important about the story is that it takes place on "Day Million," and that it is told to us directly by a narrator who informs us—not very politely—that we are primitive creatures incapable of evaluating Dora and Don's way of expressing their love. It is possible with the story to make the assumption that the theme is to be identified with the narrator's attitude. We humans have limited capabilities which prevent us from understanding and making accurate evaluations of behavior that is outside the realm of our immediate experience. On the other hand, people are concerned with a recognizable trend shared by many modern societies, the dehumanization of Man, and here we see a love affair of the future where the only contact between the two lovers after their initial meeting is by means of mechanical reproduction: "...she fits the recorded analogue of Don into the symbol manipulator, hooks herself in and turns herself on...." What are we to deduce? All of this goes to show that a piece of fiction doesn't always reveal a clear-cut position with regard to the issue that is being explored. This may be either because the writer does not make his attitude clear or because he may feel ambivalent or have mixed feelings about that issue. When this happens, it is reflected in the theme of the story. We could say that "Day Million" has one theme which expresses the idea that it is extremely difficult to evaluate behavior—even though it may be necessary to do so—because our perception is limited. That literary themes often show ambivalence is merely a reflection of the fact that in life we aren't always provided with easy answers.

Value

An author's ambivalence or non-ambivalence in attitude in a work may be determined by his or her values—the principles which he or she consciously or subconsciously holds regarding the worth of the ideas, people or actions in the narrative. The elements of science fiction literature that we have been discussing frequently offer an author the opportunity to explore or advocate values regarding the place of science in our world, the relationship between people and their technology, the concept of the alien, and the nature of the human being itself.

The whole concept of values in a piece of fiction can be rather confusing because there are many instances in which an author may write a story to entertain us without advocating a particular position or asking us to evaluate a particular set of principles. An author who writes a tale about a spaceman's battle against a one-eyed, seven-limbed creature from Mars may not consciously be "advocating" anything; he or she only knows from experience that to create an exciting story one needs strong dramatic contrasts to make it more intense.

Still the fact that an author makes certain artistic decisions purely for the sake of setting up an interesting conflict should not lull us into an easy sense that the contents do not count. The fact that our hypothetical spaceman is white and male, that he uses an atomic ray gun instead of crisis intervention techniques, and the very words used to describe these matters may indicate that, at least subconsciously, an author values certain kinds of characteristics in a human being and certain methods of dealing with critical problems. Likewise, the fact that the monster is in fact a monster, and a quite hostile one, may indicate something about the author's attitude toward the unknown.

On the other hand, none of this may be true. The author may not necessarily hold these values, but may simply be writing for an audience whom he or she feels they will appeal to. In this case, the fact that members of the audience respond by buying the book, by watching it in the theatre or on the TV screen, by recommending it to their friends, or by writing fan letters to the author, may

indicate that the audience holds these values.
Commercial television, which depends on a large
audience for its livelihood, often seems to operate with
this in mind. For example, the pilot program for the *Star
Trek* series had a female character in the second-in-
command position. NBC, which previewed the program
before test audiences of viewers, found that they had
trouble believing in a female in a leadership position, and
recommended that she be dropped. The woman who
played this role, who was liked as an actress by test
audiences, took the role of Nurse Christine Chappel, and
her vacated position was taken by Spock, who, of course,
was very successful with audiences.

However, this may oversimplify the whole
phenomenon of audience response. Perhaps a reader of
our hypothetical spaceman story knows perfectly well
that people other than young white males can deal with
serious problems, that the only answer to a threat may not
necessarily be the violent use of high technology, and that
the unknown is not always hostile; yet the story may
appeal to that part of the individual reader's psyche for
which these values, whether or not consciously held, still
hold an appeal. Our story might appeal to a reader's secret
desire to see difficult problems solved in the quickest and
most direct means possible even though he or she knows
that dealing with them in real life is a much more
complicated affair.

Nevertheless, because we recognize that life is a
complicated affair—that what we think of as evil may
have its good aspects, that what we value as good may
have its limitations, that our well-meaning actions may
have negative effects—we may discover those stories in
which these ambiguities are reflected to be more
satisfying than stories which present the world in rigid
good-evil polarities. This is, of course, true with science
fiction stories as well as with other types of fiction. If
Asimov, as a scientist, values science and the scientific
method as a "good," his story "Nightfall" shows, in

Faro's description of the failed attempt to artificially create the conditions of the coming eclipse, and in the scientists' inability to cope with the reality of their own insignificance, that science too has its limitations. Likewise, it shows that the enemies of the scientists, the Cultists, are not merely fanatics, but individuals who act on their own religious beliefs, however misguided. "Nightfall" is a good story partly because it attempts to "give the devil his due" and to show that scientists are not all-knowing, but that the scientific method is the best means limited human beings have of learning what the universe is like. Similarly, Walter Miller, Jr., in "Crucifixus Etiam," seems to hold material progress in high esteem and attempts to show that a rigid, often seemingly irrational order of discipline is necessary to create it; but by presenting the forging of a new civilization on another planet from the point of view of a common laborer working there, he does not flinch from the suffering, confusion and terror that go into its making. In fact, Miller attempts to show that the laborer's acceptance of suffering for the sake of future progress gives him dignity and maturity.

Sometimes an author may feel something is completely evil and may not be interested in exploring it in a sympathetic light. With science fiction, this is often true when an author takes a current trend and from it extrapolates a vision of what the future will be like if it continues. Stephen Vincent Benet's comically grim "Nightmare Number Three" is a good example. It is a poem narrated by an "average American" describing a revolt of machinery in New York City, and while we are not required to believe that Benet thinks it is going to happen (we hope), we still know that he has a negative attitude toward the machine-inundated civilization and the type of personality—represented by the narrator—who accepts it.

Another way of expressing a value occurs in Ursula Le Guin's "Nine Lives," which uses a story of the meeting of clones and humans to explore the ideas of human isolation and fear of the unknown other. Two men are on a distant planet in order to prospect for mineral resources. After they have lived alone for two years, a crew of assistants arrive; all are clones taken from the intestinal cells of a single being. The two men are uncomfortable; they feel "the primitive anxiety, the old dread" of meeting strangers, as the narrator says early in the story. The clones are strange; they look and think alike, they work together with machine-like efficiency, and they lack any sense of privacy, since they are essentially one person. The two groups—the men and the clones—live apart. However, an earthquake on the planet kills all the clones but one, who is nursed back to health by the two men. As this happens, the clone begins to realize that he is now a separate being who must learn to live and love as separate individuals do, and the two men begin to understand how it feels to be a clone who has lost the rest of his "self." At the end of the story, just before a new set of clones is to arrive on the planet to replace the two men, one of the men asks the remaining clone if he wishes to join the two on an exploratory mission to another planet. In a symbolic gesture, the man puts his hand on the clone's shoulder, affirming the author's central value of understanding and empathy between all of us who are physically and psychologically estranged from one another. "Nine Lives" is interesting not only because it eloquently expresses this value, but also because Le Guin convincingly and with understanding shows us the fear, the suspicion, the unexpressed wish that everyone be like oneself or one's kind, which are the basis of our more antisocial values.

As for ourselves as readers, the whole notion of values in a work of fiction may cause problems, especially if we do not share the author's values, either because we plainly disagree with them or because the story itself comes from a different time and place than our own. A strongly fundamentalist Christian may reject Asimov's

"Nightfall," for instance, because it advocates the scientific method as a surer way to truth than religious revelation. Furthermore, the story was written during the early 1940's; those who lived to see the atom bomb, bio-chemical weaponry, and other evils of applied science may today question Asimov's enthusiasm for the "advantages" science has to offer. Also, the story can be misread; for example, inexperienced readers with strong religious beliefs may feel that Asimov is really on the side of the Cultists. Letting our beliefs color our perception of what an author is saying is something that is easy for everyone; the remedy for it, which is also the remedy for the other problems mentioned, is to read the story itself carefully to understand what the author is attempting to communicate, what, in fact, the author's values really are, and to understand, if necessary, the time and place in which the story was written. Quite often, complete enjoyment of a story requires that we approach it with two minds: an objective mind, which is open to a work of literature and its values (and does not confuse them with our own), and a subjective mind, which contains our own personal response, based on our own values and experiences of life and literature. No one would suggest that we can repress our personal response to a work, or even that we should; but we should know what the author wanted us to respond to and why.

SYMBOL AND MYTH

Symbol

Symbols are devices that all of us use every day of our lives; they can be terms, names, pictures, objects. When a policeman wears a badge, he's not just wearing a piece of metal; he's wearing a symbol of authority. If a person possesses a Mercedes Benz, he's not merely the owner of a vehicle made out of metal; he possesses a symbol of wealth, status and taste. Indeed, many modern technological societies have been criticized because they seem to encourage their citizens to attain status symbols; in our country certain kinds of cars, expensive jewelry, swimming pools, fancy homes or apartments all represent—are symbolic of—wealth, status and perhaps power.

According to Suzanne Langer, a noted critic and philosopher, symbolization or the process of creating symbols is a basic need, a fundamental process which goes on all the time. This need to create symbols and strive to attain them is unique to man. Animals may compete for status—but they do not fight for symbols of status. The leader of a pack of wolves doesn't wear a crown, or feathers; nor does he require a den "in the right part of the forest." But unlike animals, men create and use symbols all of the time. Regardless of whether a culture is highly technological or quite primitive (nontechnological), the individual members create symbols regularly.

Symbols are vital to men in many ways. The most complex symbolic system that each of us uses every day of our lives is language. Every word in a language is a symbol for something. That is, the word "apple" stands for a red, juicy, hard fruit. The fruit could just as easily be called "boogle"; the French word for the fruit is "pomme." The point being made here is that so long as people agree on a particular symbol, it can be used. Speakers of a language can communicate because the meanings of the words are shared in common. There is no intrinsic rightness about calling a red, hard fruit an "apple," but if an individual chose to call it a "beek," no one would know what he/she was talking about. Since speakers of a language share a complex symbolic system, it enables them to communicate about many things, things experienced and things *not* experienced. That is one of the most wondrous things about language—it enables us to talk/think about things we never have and *never will* actually experience: voyages to distant stars, excursions to the far distant future, journeys into the minds of others.

Often symbols come into being because they help us understand many things that are unknown, hidden, vague—impossible for us to grasp. For example, consider the idea of divinity. We can give such a concept a name: God, Allah or Zeus. But it is clearly a concept beyond the grasp of reason. The more we think about divinity, the more we realize that it is beyond us. It is not at all surprising, therefore, that most religions employ symbols because these symbols enable us to reach out toward concepts that we cannot fully understand or comprehend. Christianity uses the cross to symbolize the faith itself as well as Christ; the thunderbolt is a symbol of Zeus. As an example in reverse, Islam rejects the tradition of symbolization of divinity used in most religions in order to emphasize the fact that divinity is beyond human understanding. There are no symbols of Allah in Islam.

Even though language is a symbolic system, and each word a symbol, man has the capability of making a symbol out of a symbol. Thus individual words can become symbols: a word or image is said to be symbolic when it implies something more than its conventional, obvious, specific meaning. For example, the word "snake," as it is used conventionally, refers to any member of a particular species of reptile. However, if the word "snake" is being used to suggest evil, to recall the Biblical story of Adam and Eve who were tempted by a serpent (snake), then the word has become a symbol: of evil, of temptation. This notion of the snake arises from the Judeo-Christian tradition. In other cultures, because of their shape and because many species shed their skins—suggesting a kind of death and rebirth—snakes have been used as fertility symbols. In no way does a particular word of object in itself have to be symbolic of a particular concept; the context of the symbol determines the concept signified or suggested by it.

Although the connection between symbol and concept is not absolute, certain symbols are considered to be universal. They seem to connote things that are an important part of man's experience and they are evident in nearly every culture and age. The symbolic value of these may differ from culture to culture, but the symbols are present. Symbols such as these are: the snake, dark, light, the sun, the moon, the stars and so on. Symbols can also be a product of a particular age or culture. But they don't necessarily have to be totally original; that is, they can be based on new applications or extensions of a universal symbol. For example, there are many McDonald's hamburger stands in this country and all over the world, and Golden Arches have come to be symbolic of modernity, efficiency and service to the masses. Of course, before the late 1960s double golden arches would not have suggested these concepts, although a high arch has traditionally meant an entrance into some place grand or glorious. Another symbol of modernity which probably has no connection with universal symbols is the computer.

Even though symbols are such a common part of everyday lives, they can cause confusion of interpretation or application. All of us, at one time or another, have confused a symbol for what it stands for, and we have all witnessed this kind of confusion. In the sixties, a rather turbulent decade for numerous reasons, one of the most prominent being the war in Vietnam, many Americans witnessed outbreaks of violence brought about because someone burned or attempted to burn the American flag. Of course, a flag—any flag—is merely a piece of colored cloth. But many Americans have confused the flag with their country's honor and pride. For them the flag becomes, at times, the *actual thing* that it symbolizes, thus the violent behavior associated with flag-burnings.

Since the concept of symbol is closely related to connotation and figurative language—it concerns meanings which go beyond the literal and are based on association and/or analogy—symbols are often confused with metaphors and similes. A red rose is often associated with love, beauty, sexual passion and—because a rose has thorns—the pain that often accompanies love. If I say my love is *like* a red rose, I am making a comparison which calls up these associations in the form of a simile. If I say my love is a rose, I am evoking these qualities in the form of a metaphor. But if I give my love a rose because I wish to express my feelings through it, I have made the rose a symbol, a symbol of my love.

Like figurative language, the use of symbols in a piece of literature provides great enrichment. There are several different symbolic patterns that are used in literary works which can be varied according to the taste and purpose of the individual writer.

Quite often a piece of fiction or a poem is dominated by a particular symbol; the symbol is there throughout the story, from beginning to end. An example of a dominant symbol is the symbol of the signs in the story "The Subliminal Man," by J.G. Ballard. The very first sentence of the story is, " 'The signs, Doctor. Have you seen the signs?' " The Signs are gigantic electronic billboards which subliminally (without the people knowing it) advertise a whole array of consumer goods: cigarettes, ovens, cars, televisions, and so on. Thus, every member of this rather frightening future society spends all of his/her time consuming and working, working and consuming. The signs present throughout the story are symbols of the diabolical modern, technological, materialistic society, the "rat race" in which helpless citizens spend every waking hour buying goods that they don't need and that they are manipulated into thinking they want.

Another example of a story which is dominated by a symbol is H.G. Wells' "The Star." As the title suggests, the dominant symbol within this story is a star. Briefly, the story tells of a star, which, while traveling through the universe, comes so close to earth that it causes massive upheavals on the planet (earthquakes, floods, tidal waves) and thus terrible catastrophe for all lifeforms—including people. At the beginning of the story the star is merely a "new body...rapidly growing larger and brighter" noticed by "scientific people." Even as the star becomes visible to the people, "a great white star...brighter than any other," most are still too caught up in their day-to-day existence to give it much more attention than a casual glance or a passing remark. As the story progresses there are exceptions, though. A mathematician looks up at the star and says, "You may kill me....But I can hold you—and all the universe for that matter—in the grip of this little brain. I would not change. Even now." Thus the star is initially a symbol of the unknown, a symbol of all that is "out there" yet seldom thought about, seldom feared because it is not a part of everyday immediate experience. By the end of the story, after the star has caused so much destruction, it has come to be a symbol not only of the unknown but of the unknown become knowable—a bringer of terrible suffering, agony and wonder.

Sometimes a symbol is not entirely evident early in the story, but develops as the story unfolds. An example is the evolution of Manue Nanti into a symbol of the Christ figure in the story "Crucifixus Etiam." The title of the story gives the reader a clue that something of this nature might occur. "Crucifixus Etiam," which means "He was crucified also," is taken from the Nicene Creed, a central part of Catholic and most Protestant services. The Nicene Creed is a declaration of faith in the basic tenets of Christianity as those particular sects see them. The story is about the sacrifices being made by workers on the planet Mars so that the atmosphere will become breathable for human beings in eight hundred years. In the meantime, those who prepare the way for others must live under extreme conditions of hardship and rely on mechanical oxygenators to be able to breath. Manue Nanti makes a commitment to the future of humanity by deciding to spend his life on Mars working on the project; such a commitment requires the sacrifice of his lungs, since relying on the oxygenator for any lenth of time causes them to atrophy. He can never return to Earth again. As the story continues, Manue experiences a struggle and agony, which are made to seem similar to those of Christ. Manue's period of agony leading up to his understanding and acceptance of his sacrifice is described as "Manue's desperate Gethsemane." He too in the end sacrifices himself for a great purpose: "He knew what Mars was—not a ten-thousand-a-year job, not a garbage can for surplus production. But an eight-century passion of human faith in the destiny of Man." All through the story references are made which establish Manue as a Christ symbol, a symbol of supreme sacrifice for the love of man. The above-quoted passage, taken from the end of the story, brings to mind through the word "passion" the passion of Christ, His suffering—Man's redemption.

Many works do not contain a dominant symbol; they may, however, contain more contextual symbols that provide enrichment. Furthermore, even if a story, poem or play does contain a dominant symbol, oftentimes there are many symbols within the story that contribute to the dominant symbol and to the story. For example, if a story has a character who symbolizes a Christ figure, it is not unusual to find images and events within the story symbolizing those things associated with Christ: the cross, Calvary, the cup used at the Last Supper, the Last Supper itself, and so on. Sometimes symbols within a work can provide enrichment by helping set the tone or foreshadowing events to come. A good example of symbolic foreshadowing can be found in the novel *The Invincible,* by Stanislaw Lem. The Invincible is a starship with a crew of eighty-three men sent to investigate what happened to an earlier ship, the Condor, which never returned home. By the end of the novel, the mystery of the Condor is solved and it also becomes clear (at least to the reader) that man is an unwelcome intruder on the planet, the cause of his own destruction. In the early pages of the novel there are several symbolic foreshadowings, but the most dramatic is the description of the ship as the landing party disembarks:

As they crept out from under the ship's stern, he [Rohan, the central character] noticed the gigantic shadow cast by the "Invincible" ahead of them, a dark road stretched straight out across the sand dunes, bathed in the light of the setting sun. . . .[The] warm, delicate pink reminded him of the pastel hues he had seen in picture books as a child. Such incredibly soft colors.

The shadow cast by the ship, a darkness thrust upon an idyllic landscape, symbolizes the intrusion of man and foreshadows the destruction that is to come—man has created his own "dark road."

Often a series of interrelated symbols can function together within a particular work to create additional meanings. Herman Melville's "The Tartarus of Maids" concerns the visit of the narrator, a businessman, to a paper mill in New England in order to arrange for the purchase of paper. Even at first glance the story is a rather obvious attack on the labor practices of the period, especially the treatment of women, who make up the labor force of the mills. The narrator is conducted on a guided tour of the mill, which includes a room where, "like so many mares haltered to the rack, stood rows of girls," cutting rags into small pieces in preparation for the pulp vats. The cutting process also produces lint: "The air swam with the fine, poisonous particles, which from all sides darted, subtilely, as motes in sunbeams, into the lungs." Additional details are present throughout the story reinforcing the impression that mills such as this one are for women a true Hell (Tartarus was the abode of evil-doers in the afterlife in ancient Greek mythology).

But other kinds of details suggest that at work in the story is an additional symbolic theme, which is revealed especially in the description of "the great machine...which makes the paper." It begins with vats of pulp, "a white, wet, wooly-looking stuff, not unlike the albuminous part of an egg, soft-boiled." The pulp pours from the vats down a channel into "a room, stifling with abdominal heat, as if here, true enough, were being developed the germinous particles lately seen." Thence it is progressively rolled out in a machine described as "one continuous length of iron framework—multitudinous and mystical, with all sorts of rollers, wheel, and cylinders."

The comparison with an egg and the mention of "germinous particles" being shaped in "abdominal heat" in a machine "multitudinous and mystical" might already suggest to some readers a similarity between this description and that of the development of a human being in a mother's womb. On the other hand, many readers at this point in the story might consider such a comparison far-fetched, but the similarities continue to develop. The narrator asks how long it takes for the pulp to go through the machine. The answer is "only nine minutes." At the other end of the machine is "a sad-looking woman...an elder person...silently tending the machine-end." She functions symbolically as a mid-wife, a point reinforced by the fact that she is described as having formerly been a nurse; into her hands "the piles of moist, warm sheets...continually were delivered." Indeed, Melville is

not subtle about the comparison at this point. His
narrator goes on to wonder, as one might wonder about
new-born human beings, "of those strange uses to which
those thousand sheets eventually would be put. All sorts
of writings would be writ on those now vacant things." If
any doubt remains, the narrator, apparently in all
innocence, makes the comparison explicit:

I could not but bethink me of that celebrated comparison of John
Locke [an eighteenth-century British philosopher], who, in
demonstration of this theory that man had no innate ideas,
compared the human mind at birth to a sheet of blank paper;
something destined to be scribbled on, but what sort of
characters no soul might tell.

At this point we might also remember details which
turned up earlier in the story without apparent purpose:
the fact that the narrator's guide through the mill is a boy
strangely called Cupid, after the Greek god of love; the
fact that the mill is powered by "the turbid waters of Blood
River"; the fact that the narrator is in "the seedsman's
business," needing paper for seed packs; and many more.
     It would be easy for readers to get carried away in
symbol-hunting expeditions and find questionable
second meanings everywhere (indeed, many professional
critics have done so). But so consistent a set of
correspondences as can be found in the Melville story
suggests that the author was consciously and deliberately
creating the correspondences. But for what purpose does
the paper mill become a symbol of the human womb?
     The answers to such questions are not always certain
or clear, but it is important to realize that the discovery of
a symbolic level of meaning does not nullify the more
obvious surface meaning. Our reading "at first glance"
was by no means wrong; this is still a story attacking the
abuse of women in the nineteenth-century labor market
(the story was first published in 1855). But perhaps it also
suggests the abuse of women by the universe itself in
another labor market, that of childbirth. Perhaps the

second Tartarus of maids is women's condemnation to the task of reproducing the race, the futility of which is emphasized by the fact that the primary product of the mill is "foolscap," a suggestive technical name for a common kind of writing paper. Other concepts associated with childbearing, especially in the nineteenth century, connect with the plight of the mill workers in the story: the high incidence of women's deaths in childbirth and the social pressures emphasizing childbearing as the primary function of women. Other connections may be found, perhaps further whole complexes of meaning. Symbols become ways to suggest multiple levels of meaning, not only within a single image, but in whole series of images.

No matter what sort of symbolic pattern a writer decides to use, there are many options as to the source of symbols. Sometimes a writer might choose to incorporate traditional symbols into his work, symbols like the snake, the sun, the moon, the stars, the coming of spring (often symbolic of new life, rebirth), etc. Or an author might choose to use contemporary symbols like McDonald's golden arches, a gold Cadillac, a flag, a military uniform, a driver's license (often used as a symbol of coming of age since licenses are awarded to sixteen-year-olds). Whether a symbol is used as expected or turned around is determined by the intent of the artist. For example, the snake—usually symbolic of evil and temptation in the Judeo-Christian tradition—might be symbolic of innocence and purity in a particular work. In such a case, the alteration of the reader's expectations about the use of the symbol could help to strengthen and enrich the theme of the work, it could contribute to irony, or it could contribute to a comic effect, and so on. In any event, the alteration of an expected pattern is a common literary technique, whether relating to plot structure, characterization, use of symbols, or whatever.

Another option a writer has with regard to symbol usage is to create one or some of his/her own. This practice can often be quite intriguing because, although a "new" symbol doesn't have the rich tradition associated with commonly used symbols, a symbol that is skillfully created *for* a particular work has a unique organic relationship to it. An example of a symbol that was created for a story is the use of signs in J.G. Ballard's "The Subliminal Man."

Science fiction often uses symbols uniquely because of the ways it can literalize metaphors and turn them into symbols. Most of us have felt at one time or another that the social system was turning us into numbers; science fiction can literalize the metaphor and create a world in which all people are indeed identified only by numbers. If machines seem to have a mind of their own at times, science fiction can create worlds in which machines in fact do. The metaphor, "Life is a bowl of cherries," could conceivably be literalized into a story about a planet shaped rather like a bowl with red and round and juicy inhabitants—rather like cherries. Thus the planet would symbolize an existence representative or illustrative of the sentiment being expressed in the saying. In fact, Philip Jose Farmer does something similar in his story, "A Bowl Bigger than Earth." The setting of the story is a hell-like planet which, as the story progresses, becomes strongly suggestive of a toilet bowl.

Myth

Myths are the oldest stories known to man, usually distinguished from literary art as most of us know it because most myths are older than writing and because myths are usually seen as the creations and property of a whole culture rather than of any individual author. Since the latter part of the nineteenth century, there has been in Western culture a great deal of interest in and study of myth, an interest that has been illuminating in its discoveries of new information and bewildering in its production of numerous contradictory theories by the philosophers, theologians, psychologists, anthropologists, linguists and literary critics who have approached the topic with sometimes widely varying assumptions and perspectives.

The reasons for all this interest are many, but they begin in the nineteenth century with a problem and a pair of initial discoveries. The problem concerns the conviction among many people that modern science was demythologizing the world, turning all the old faiths and the narratives that expressed and supported them into mere fictions, the products of simple, childish and superstitious minds. It is this antipathetic attitude that created the popular misunderstanding that myths are lies or old beliefs exposed as false. (As scholars use it and as it is used here, myth carries no implication of truth or falsity; we can speak of the Christian myth without implying any judgment of it.) Many people, however, regretted the passing of the myths and felt there was something profound, important and vital about them without which modern life was turning sterile, empty and meaningless. This is a feeling that has continued unabated, indeed intensified, throughout the twentieth century.

The initial discoveries which stimulated further interest were two. The first was the growing realization by folklorists and anthropologists like the brothers Wilhelm and Jacob Grimm (the collectors of the well-known *Grimm's Fairy Tales*) that the myths and folktales of widely separated cultures bear striking similarities to one another. The second was the discovery by psychoanalysts, especially Sigmund Freud, that people's dreams bear striking similarities to myths and folktales.

The possible implications of these discoveries and their connections with the problem of the lack of myth in the modern age are so many that only a few can be mentioned here. First, perhaps the myths are not dead at all, but still alive in our subconscious minds; the world of myth emerges for us every night when we dream. And perhaps, instead of seeing ourselves as too civilized for that sort of thing, we actually need to pay more attention to the non-rational parts of our being like myths and dreams. Myths, like dreams, may offer insight into fundamental ways in which our own mind and the human mind in general work, since, indeed, myths seem to be public dreams just as dreams are private myths.

Freud tended to see dreams and myths as manifestations of mental disorder, maladjustments, but later scholars like C.G. Jung and Joseph Campbell saw myth as an expression of an active, vital and healthy mind, as

the secret opening through which the inexhaustible energies of the cosmos pour into human cultural manifestations. Religions, philosophies, arts, the social forms of primitive historic man, prime discoveries in science and technology, the very dreams that blister sleep, boil up from the basic, magic ring of myth (Joseph Campbell, *The Hero with A Thousand Faces,* New York: Pantheon, 1949).

Examples of how so many things can boil up are numerous, but one of especial relevance is the process of literary creation itself. We have discussed in the section on Symbol how an author consciously creates and builds up a pattern of symbols, but it is not at all uncommon for readers to discover symbolic patterns in a work of art which the author will admit are there but which he had no awareness of having consciously created. Indeed, the whole idea of artistic inspiration comes from the experience shared by many artists of being taken over by the work so that the story or poem seemed to write itself. The writer thus feels himself to be not so much a creator as a medium through which something else worked—God, the creative process itself, the unconscious—whatever.

There is, therefore, a process of creation, of meaningful patterning and structuring, which seems to operate on the unconscious level. Moreover, the fact that myth and literature can move us so deeply may have something to do with their exhibition of symbolic images and patterns shared by the unconscious minds of all of us;

they create in us a mysterious sense of recognition by striking a responsive chord deep within us. Jung called these universally shared symbols *archetypes* (images such as water, whether in the form of the sea, or of rivers, the sun, the earth, and the moon, the garden and the desert, father figures, both destructive and caring, Earth mothers and terrible mothers, and many more; patterns like the hero stories of quest, initiation, or sacrificial scapegoat). Jung saw these archetypes as emerging out of a collective unconscious, a storehouse of symbolic forms held in common by all human minds, as much a part of the inborn structure of the mind as heart, liver, bone and muscle are parts of the structure of the body.

However far one wishes to push the significance of myth, modern literature has nevertheless been greatly influenced by myth and myth theories, and science fiction, which Northrup Frye describes as "a mode of romance with a strong inherent tendency to myth" (*The Anatomy of Criticism,* Princeton: Princeton University Press, 1957), reveals a similar influence.

Myths can be found in literature in a number of ways. One of the most basic in science fiction is the story which "explains" a mythical event or demonstrates the "fact" behind the myth. There are many stories built around a visit to Earth thousands of years ago by advanced extraterrestrials, which becomes to human witnesses the basis for a mythical story of a visit by a god. Arthur C. Clarke offers a different kind of explanation for a myth in "The Star," which concerns a priest who accompanies an interstellar expedition that discovers the remains of the sun which went nova and produced the star of Bethlehem. The story centers on the additional and more disturbing discovery that the stellar explosion had destroyed a highly advanced civilization close to the exploded sun; the priest is confronted with the ironic fact that the "star" which announced man's salvation had meant the doom of a whole world.

These stories could be called anti-myths, stories

which deny or call into question the traditional meaning of particular myths. Another example of a different kind of anti-myth is Archibald MacLeish's poem "The End of the World," which was discussed in the section on Setting. It counts for much of its ironic effect on our expectation of the end of the world producing monumental, mythical events like graves opening up and Christ coming in clouds of glory to judge the living and the dead. Instead, "There in the sudden blackness the black pall" is "nothing, nothing, nothing—nothing at all."

Not all retellings of myths are antithetical to them, however. In *Perelandra* C.S. Lewis tells a story set in an Eden-like Venus, where another Adam and Eve experience the temptations of Satan and this time, with the help of Ransom, an appropriately named human, obey God's command, do not eat of the Tree of the Knowledge of Good and Evil, and do not fall.

There are also stories which, without retelling or explaining a myth, make use of one as a kind of symbolic background. This technique is evident in the subtitle of Mary Shelley's *Frankenstein, or The Modern Prometheus*. Prometheus was the rebel god who, against Zeus' orders, took compassion on man, stole fire from the gods, gave it to man, and suffered dire punishment for it. Shelley, however, presents the Prometheus figure more in terms of his Christian counterpart, Satan. His angelic name, Lucifer, meaning light-bearer, links him closely with Prometheus, but Satan's rebellion against God is seen as purely evil. Indeed, the scientist in science fiction is most typically presented in these larger-than-life, mythic terms, either as the Promethean rebel-savior, struggling against the "old gods," the old religious or intellectual order, and bringing the redemptive light of new knowledge to mankind, or as the Satanic rebel who, in his proud and ruthless quest for knowledge and power, causes terrible evil to mankind.

Ray Bradbury can be seen as making use of a powerful mythic symbol in "Here There Be Tygers," where a human expedition visits a plant, the whole of which is a single sentient being, feminine in personality. She is a literal living manifestation of the mythic figure of the Earth Mother, especially reminiscent of the Earth Mother among Amerindian tribes; these tribes resisted the white man's attempts to convert them from hunters to farmers because it was against their religion; they believed that it was proper to take from their mother the Earth only what she freely gave, the plants and animals that grew of themselves on her bosom. To dig into her skin and force her to yield her fruits (which a character in the Bradbury story tries to do more violently with a mining machine) they saw as a kind of rape. This similarity is relevant to Bradbury's story since it carries an ecological theme and emphasizes the importance of treating a planet with the consideration due a person, even the reverence due a loving mother. Indeed, the literal image of the living earth presented in the story is probably as close as modern man can come to expressing that primeval consciousness in which the Earth was experienced as a living being.

Works of fiction may also employ myth in the form of *patterns* such as those mentioned earlier, stories of quest, initiation and sacrificial scapegoat. We can show how some of these patterns work by examining part of what Joseph Campbell sees as a single, elaborate, overriding "monomyth," the one archetypal pattern of departure, initiation and return, which sums up the paths of all heroes and of which all myths are a part. Here are the bare bones of the monomyth as Campbell describes it in *The Hero With a Thousand Faces*:

A hero ventures forth from the world of common day into a region of supernatural wonder: fabulous forces are there encountered and a decisive victory is won: the hero comes back from this mysterious adventure with the power to bestow boons on his fellow man.

The purpose of analyzing a specific work of art in terms of

such a pattern is to help account for at least something of the special kind of almost magical effect that certain works seem to produce. For example, one of the most popular science fiction novels in recent years is Frank Herbert's *Dune,* a novel which very clearly centers on a hero figure and lends itself especially well to analysis in terms of its exhibition of features of the monomyth. So numerous are the correspondences, in fact, that it would be prohibitive to explore them all in this context, but there is time and space to look at a few.

Consider the opening paragraph of the novel:

In the week before their departure to Arrakis, when all the final scurrying about had reached a nearly unbearable frenzy, an old crone came to visit the mother of the boy Paul.

The departure, the first stage in the departure, initiation and return pattern, begins, according to Campbell, with a "call to action," announced by a herald of the adventure who is often dark, loathly or terrifying. This function is performed in *Dune* by the old crone, who is described in terms which recall similar figures in folktales: "The old woman was a witch shadow—hair like matted spiderwebs, hooded 'round darkness of features, eyes like glittering jewels."

Indeed, there is in a sense more than one call to adventure in *Dune*. The first has already happened as the story opens, the change in the fortunes of Paul's father which necessitates a move from the family's comfortable home planet, "the world of common day" in Campbell's words, to a perilous new domain, the planet Arrakis or Dune, the Desert planet, a world that will gradually reveal near supernatural wonders. The second call happens more directly to young Paul, for the old crone turns out to be the powerful head, "the Reverend Mother," of a secret, priest-like society of women, of which Paul's mother is a member. The Reverend Mother goes on to subject Paul to a painful test, which he passes, but as a result, "Paul felt that he had been infected with a terrible purpose. He did not know yet what that terrible purpose was." The situation and language could almost be seen as echoing Campbell's summary of the first step in the hero's journey, the call to action, which "signifies that destiny has summoned the hero and transferred his spiritual center of gravity from within the pale of his society to a zone unknown."

The stage of departure culminates in an initial threshhold experience, which for Paul culminates in the betrayal and death of his father and his flight with his mother into exile in the desert, a crossing of a threshold by which Paul moves into the second broad stage of the hero pattern, initiation.

Initiation is typically presented in terms of some kind of symbolic death-rebirth pattern, perhaps because the human mind imagines major change as the death of the old and the birth of the new. Within myths and folktales such changes take place in a region of both supernatural wonder and natural trial and testing, most typically a dark wood or a desert, an underground world or sometimes the very insides of a terrible monster. It is necessary for the hero to pass through this region and its trials in order to achieve his ultimate transformation, his rebirth, into the god or god-like figure who can return with "the power to bestow boons to his fellow man."

The tests and trials the hero might undergo are many, but Paul manages to experience most of the possibilities: personal combat in hand-to-hand battle to the death, and the subduing or slaying of a terrible monster (in Paul's case, riding the frightful sandworm). Paul's last and most desperate trial is partaking of "the Water of Death, (water is an archetypal symbol of death and rebirth, which is why it is the most important symbol in the Christian ritual of Baptism). The Water of Death casts Paul into an extended death-like trance and brings about a final awakening of new awareness and understanding. This experience completes Paul's initiation, which clearly exhibits the death-rebirth pattern and demonstrates finally that Paul is the messiah the desert people have been long awaiting.

The hero's return is still to come, but the purpose of this discussion is not a thorough analysis of the mythic patterns in *Dune*—indeed we have only scratched the surface—rather to present just enough of an indication to show that mythic patterns are decidedly there. Much remains for the reader to entertain himself filling in, in the way not only of general mythic images and patterns, but also of more specific ones, allusions to and parallels with Moses, Christ, especially Mohammed, and many others. But the special effectiveness of the use of mythic patterns does not depend on the reader's recognition of specific parallels and mythical allusions; rather it depends on the reinforcement of the reader's unconscious response, the expectation that such patterns will of themselves profoundly move the reader, creating a sense of identity between the hero of fiction and the archetypal hero pattern that exists in the collective unconscious of us all.

This concept of the collective unconscious is certainly a debatable one, and there are anthropologists who argue that both Jung and Campbell have overemphasized the universality of the archetypes. Yet the unusual success of works like *Dune*, which so strongly makes use of mythic patterns and images, would suggest that there is still great power of some kind behind mythic patterns.

Nevertheless, there are important ways in which myth can be seen not only as an expression of universal human experience but as an expression of the world vision and historical sense of a particular culture. An especially interesting example, and one which also illustrates the fact that myths need not be ancient, is the subject of a book by Richard Slotkin, *Regeneration Through Violence: The Mythology of the American Frontier, 1600-1860* (Middleton, Conn.: Wesleyan University Press, 1973). Slotkin argues that, while employing the basic archetypal patterns and images, "various cultures move away from the universal vision of the archetype toward some particular interpretation of the archetypal narrative that will reflect their characteristic approach to life." Thus it is that "myth provides a useful tool for the analysis of the particularity of a human culture."

Slotkin examines how there gradually developed from the Colonial period through the nineteenth century a typically American version of the archetypal pattern based upon the frontier experience. As one might imagine, in popular narratives of the frontier experience the wilderness became the archetypal region of supernatural wonder where the hero's initiation took place. There developed, however, a pair of contrasting myths, in the first of which the wilderness was truly the dark wood, the hellish abode of devilish savages. It was the hero's task, if he or she became their captive (a woman was often the hero of captivity narratives), to resist their temptations and remain uncorrupted by the powers of darkness; otherwise it was the hero's task to convert or destroy them. In the second contrasting myth, the wilderness was the abode of noble savages, honest, sexually uninhibited and free of the corruptions of the old world; the wilderness itself was a land rich with the promise to European man of renewal and rebirth, of both spiritual and erotic regeneration; in this myth the hero's task was to become one with the wilderness through a sacred marriage with an Indian maiden who symbolized the spirit of the wilderness. These opposing myths Slotkin sees as being reconciled in the major American myth, which he calls the hunter myth, the myth of regeneration through violence. This myth presents the hero as a hunter who paradoxically was a lover of the spirit of the wilderness, yet whose "acts of love and sacred affirmation" were most typically "acts of violence against that spirit." The violence was typically justified by the need to free the white captive (usually a beautiful woman) and by the promise of opening up the wilderness to the higher cultivation of the white settler. In simplest terms, this means that the American myth encouraged, even justified, the expression of love of the wilderness by expropriation and exploitation of the land and near extermination of its original inhabitants: "The hunter myth imagines the relationship between man and nature (or man and god) as that of hunter to prey; and the final expression of such a relationship is the domination, destruction and absorption of one by the other."

The relevance of this kind of mythological approach to science fiction derives, of course, from the fact that some of its most typical settings, outer space and other planets, are new frontiers in which both author and reader have the opportunity to recreate or reassess our frontier experience. And science fiction has done both. It has recreated the American myth in novels and stories ranging from E.E. Smith's Skylark and Lensmen series to Robert A. Heinlein's *Starship Troopers,* works which present the human race as the noble opponents of evil alien creatures "out there," since we are the beings destined to conquer the universe; this is science fiction's version of the nineteenth century American concept of Manifest Destiny. As in the hunter myth, the heroes of such stories are filled with a sense of wonder before the universe, expressing their love of its spirit, yet they typically develop a relationship with the universe in terms of metaphors of mastery, control and conquest, either by their overwhelming nobility or by their technological skills (good old yankee know-how and ingenuity) or by both.

On the other hand, science fiction, especially in the last two decades, has also reassessed the American myth and critically examined its patterns and the values and assumptions behind it. Bradbury's "Here There Be Tygers" blatantly attacks the myth, opening the story with an extreme statement of the philosophy of conquest by Chatterton, an enemy of the spirit of the wilderness and the villain of the story:

> You have to beat a planet at its own game. . . . Get in and rip it up, kill its snakes, poison its animals, dam its rivers, sow its fields, depollinate its air, mine it, nail it down, hack away at it, and get the blazes out from under when you have what you want.

Chatterton goes on to attempt a symbolic rape of the land, but this time the land is sentient, can fight back, and takes revenge. A more elaborate study from Bradbury's pen is *The Martian Chronicles,* which presents the human settlement of Mars as a reenactment of the patterns of waste, destruction and conquest that characterized man's conquest of Earth in general and especially of America.

Robert Silverberg's "Sundance" is concerned less with the land of an alien planet than with its possibly sentient inhabitants, whom the humans are in the process of exterminating. Silverberg reassesses the American myth by looking at analogous events through the eyes of Tom Two Ribbons, an Amerindian human. But Silverberg goes far deeper into the effects of myth on human beings by introducing the questions of Tom's sanity and whether he is seeing truly or projecting into the situation unresolved personal conflicts of his own.

A myth is not only the embodiment in symbolic narrative of the values and assumptions of a culture, but a means by which the members of a culture structure their personal and collective lives. One of the problems of such a process of living the myth is revealed in Tom's case: he may be imposing the Amerindian view of the American myth on a situation where it is not appropriate. As Slotkin puts it,

Through myths the psychology and world view of our cultural ancestors are transmitted to modern descendants, in such a way and with such power that our perception of contemporary reality and our ability to function in the world are directly, often tragically affected.

Slotkin later clarifies what he means by tragic effects when he argues that President Lyndon Johnson justified the escalation of the Vietnam War in metaphors drawn directly out of the hunter myth, a classic case of the inappropriate application of a mythic structure. Simple South Vietnamese farmers were seen like frontier settlers as the innocent victims of savage figures whom it was the destiny of the American hunter-hero to subdue and destroy; this destruction was justified not only by the noble effort to free the "captives," but also by the dedication of the hunter to the opening up of the forest to higher cultivation, the promise that once the Communist menace was destroyed, the land would be given the boon of America's technological know-how and become a peaceful and productive promised land.

The error was not merely presidential, however, but national. Johnson was not so much foisting the myth upon us as demonstrating that the myth embodied the value structure in terms of which he—and we—saw and felt: he said what we wanted to hear.

Important longer works worth examining in mythic terms are James Blish's *A Case of Conscience,* Philip Jose Farmer's *Dare,* Ursula Le Guin's *The Word for World is Forest,* Stanislaw Lem's *The Invincible,* and Gene Wolfe's *The Fifth Head of Cerberus.* But no matter how myths are seen as functioning in literature, whether as means to strenthen a symbolic theme, to embody cultural beliefs and values or the wisdom of the ages, or to examine critically the human or national psyche and their values, myth remains a powerful force operating in literature and life in ways of which we need to be aware.

Appendix A

A BIBLIOGRAPHY OF SHORT FICTION AND POETRY CITED, WITH LOCATION NOTES

Asimov, Isaac. "Nightfall." AARI, MOI, MSF, SFHF1, TTT.*
_____. "Runaround." ATBT, IR.
Ballard, J.G. "The Subliminal Man." MOI, TTT.
Benet, Stephen Vincent. "By the Waters of Babylon." SPEC, TOC.
_____. "Nightmare Number Three." SPEC.
Blish, James. "Common Time." MOI.
Borges, Jorge Luis. "The House of Asterion." LA.
Bradbury, Ray. "Here There Be Tygers." TTT.
_____. "The Veldt." BBST, TTT.
Brown, Fredric. "Arena." SFHF1, TTT.
Byron, George Gordon, Lord. "Darkness." ASF, NAEL3.
Campbell, John W. "Who Goes There?" ASF, SFHF2A.
Clarke, Arthur C. "The History Lesson." OSF, SFTF.
_____. "The Nine Billion Names of God." ASF, IDA, SFHF1.
_____. "The Sentinel." ATBT, MOI, TTT.
cummings, e.e. "pity this busy monster, manunkind." EEC, SAM, SPEC.
Ellison, Harlan. " 'Repent, Harlequin!' Said the Ticktockman." ATBT, IDA, SFTF, SPEC, TTT.
Forster, E.M. "The Machine Stops." SFHF2B, SFTF.
Godwin, Tom. "The Cold Equations." ASF, IDA, MSF, SFHF1.
Heinlein, Robert A. "The Roads Must Roll." FSFS, SFHF1.
Hickey, James. "Gone are the Lupo." Q1.
Keyes, Daniel. "Flowers for Algernon." BFSF9,HW1, SFHF1.
Le Guin, Ursula. "Nine Lives." ASF, ATBT, IDA, MSF, TWC.
Leinster, Murray. "First Contact." AARI, ASF, SFHF1.
Lovecraft, H.P. "The Colour Out of Space." IDA, OSF.
MacLeish, Archibald. "The End of the World." IP, NAMP.

124

Melville, Herman. "The Tartarus of Maids." IDA, SPEC.
Miller, Walter, Jr. "Crucifixus Etiam." TTT.
Pohl, Frederick. "Day Million." SFA, SFTF, TWC.
Russ, Joanna. "When It Changed." ADV.
Sheckley, Robert. "Specialist." ATBT, MOI, TTT.
Shelley, Percy Bysshe. "Ozymandias." IP, NAEL3, SAM.
Silverberg, Robert. "Sundance." SPEC, TTT, TWC.
Simak, Clifford. "A Death in the House." ATBT, SFBB.
———. "Desertion." BBSF, TTT.
Smith, Cordwainer. "The Game of Rat and Dragon." ATBT, MOI, SFA.
Sturgeon, Theodore. "Slow Sculpture." NAS6, SPEC.
Thomas, D.M. "Tithonus." SFTF.
Vogt, A.E. van. "The Weapon Shop." SFHF1.
Weinbaum, Stanley G. "A Martian Odyssey." SFHF1.
Wells, H.G. "The Star." ASF, MOI, TTT.
Wolfe, Gene. "Eyebem." O7.
———. "The Island of Dr. Death and Other Stories." NAS6, O7.
Zelazny, Roger. "A Rose for Ecclesiastes." BFSF14, SFHF1, SFTF.

*See Key to Anthologies and Collections for identification of abbreviations.

KEY TO ANTHOLOGIES AND COLLECTIONS

AARI Harrison, Harry, and Brian Aldiss, eds. *The Astounding-Analog Reader*. Vol. I. New York: Doubleday, 1972.

ADV Ellison, Harlan, ed. *Again, Dangerous Visions, I*. New York: Doubleday, 1972; rpt. New York: Signet, 1973.

ASF Lawler, Donald L., ed. *Approaches to Science Fiction*. Boston: Houghton Mifflin, 1978.

ATBT Sullivan, Charles William, III, ed. *As Tomorrow Becomes Today*. Englewood Cliffs, NJ: Prentice-Hall, 1974.

BBSF Conklin, Groff, ed. *The Big Book of Science Fiction*. New York: Crown, 1950.

BBST Merril, Judith, ed. *Beyond the Barriers of Space and Time*. New York: Random House, 1954.

BFSF9 Mills, Robert P., ed. *The Best from Fantasy and Science Fiction*. Series 9. New York: Doubleday, 1960.

BFSF14 Davidson, Avram, ed. *The Best from Fantasy and Science Fiction*. Series 14. New York: Doubleday, 1965.

EEC cummings, e.e. *E.E. Cummings' Poems: 1923-1954*. New York: Harcourt Brace, 1954.

FSFS Healy, Raymond J., and J. Francis McComas, eds. *Famous Science Fiction Stories: Adventures in Time and Space*. New York: Modern Library, 1946.

HW1 Asimov, Isaac, ed. *The Hugo Winners*. Vol. 1. Garden City, NY: Doubleday, 1962; rpt. Greenwich, CT: Fawcett, 1973.

IDA Fiedler, Leslie A., ed. *In Dreams Awake: A Historical-Critical Anthology of Science Fiction*. New York: Dell, 1975.

IP	Kennedy, X.J., ed. *An Introduction to Poetry.* 3rd ed. Boston: Little, Brown, 1966.
IR	Asimov, Isaac. *I, Robot.* New York: Doubleday, 1950; rpt. Greenwich, CT: Fawcett, 1970.
LA	Borges, Jorge Luis. *Labyrinths: Selected Stories and Other Writings.* New York: New Directions, 1964.
MOI	Silverberg, Robert, ed. *The Mirror of Infinity: A Critics' Anthology of Science Fiction.* New York: Harper & Row, 1970.
MSF	Spinrad, Norman, ed. *Modern Science Fiction.* New York: Doubleday, 1974.
NAEL3	Abrams, M.H., *et al,* eds. *The Norton Anthology of English Literature.* 3rd ed. Vol. 2. New York: Norton, 1972.
NAMP	Ellmann, Richard, and Robert Oclair, eds. *The Norton Anthology of Modern Poetry.* New York: Norton, 1973.
NAS6	Simak, Clifford D., ed. *Nebula Award Stories Six.* Garden City, NY: Doubleday, 1971.
O7	Knight, Damon, ed. *Orbit 7.* New York: Putnam; New York: Berkley, 1970.
OSF	Conklin, Groff, ed. *The Omnibus of Science Fiction.* New York: Crown, 1952.
Q1	Delany, Samuel R., and Marilyn Hacker, eds. *Quark 1.* New York: Paperback Library, 1970.
SAM	Dube, Anthony, *et al,* eds. *Structure and Meaning: An Introduction to Literature.* Boston: Houghton Mifflin, 1976.
SFA	Knight, Damon, ed. *A Science Fiction Argosy.* New York: Simon and Schuster, 1972.
SFBB	Merril, Judith, ed. *SF: The Best of the Best.* New York: Delacorte, 1967.
SFHF1	Silverberg, Robert, ed. *The Science Fiction Hall of Fame: The Greatest Science Fiction Stories of All Time.* Vol. 1. New York: Doubleday, 1970; rpt. New York: Avon, 1971.
SFHF2A	Bova, Ben, ed. *The Science Fiction Hall of Fame: The Greatest Science Fiction Novellas of all Time.* Vol. 2A. New York: Doubleday, 1973; rpt. New York: Avon, 1974.

SFHF2B   Bova, Ben, ed. *The Science Fiction Hall of Fame: The Greatest Science Fiction Novellas of All Time.* Vol. 2B. New York: Doubleday, 1973; rpt. New York: Avon, 1974.

SFTF   Allen, Dick, ed. *Science Fiction: The Future.* New York: Harcourt Brace, 1971.

SPEC   Sanders, Thomas E., ed. *Speculations: An Introduction to Literature Through Fantasy and Science Fiction.* New York: Glencoe, 1973.

TOC   Benet, Stephen Vincent. *Thirteen O'Clock: Stories of Several Worlds.* Freeport, NY: Books for Libraries, 1937.

TTT   Heintz, Bonnie L., *et al,* eds. *Tomorrow, and Tomorrow, and Tomorrow....* New York: Holt, Rinehart, 1974.

TWC   Wilson, Robin Scott, ed. *Those Who Can: A Science Fiction Reader.* New York: Mentor, 1973.

128

Appendix B

A CRITICAL BIBLIOGRAPHY OF SCIENCE FICTION

Aldiss, Brian. *Billion Year Spree: The True History of Science Fiction.* Garden City, NY: Doubleday, 1973.

————, and Harry Harrison, eds. *Hell's Cartographers: Some Personal Histories of Science Fiction Writers.* New York: Harper & Row, 1976.

Amis, Kingsley. *New Maps of Hell: A Survey of Science Fiction.* New York: Harcourt Brace, 1960.

Armytage, W.H.G. *Yesterday's Tomorrows: A Historical Survey of Future Societies.* London: Routledge, 1961.

Atheling, William, Jr. (pseud. James Blish). *The Issue at Hand: Studies in Contemporary Magazine Science Fiction, 1952-1963.* Chicago: Advent, 1964.

————. *More Issues at Hand.* Chicago: Advent, 1970.

Bailey, J.O. *Pilgrims Through Space and Time: Trends and Patterns in Scientific and Utopian Fiction.* New York: Argus, 1947; rpt. Westport, CT: Greenwood, 1972.

Barron, Neil, ed. *Anatomy of Wonder: Science Fiction.* New York: Bowker, 1976.

Berger, Harold L. *Science Fiction and the New Dark Age.* Bowling Green, OH: Bowling Green Popular Press, 1976.

Bretnor, Reginald, ed. *Modern Science Fiction: Its Meaning and Future.* New York: Coward-McCann, 1953.

————. *Science Fiction Today and Tomorrow.* Baltimore, MD: Penguin, 1974.

————. *The Craft of Science Fiction.* New York: Harper & Row, 1976.

Clareson, Thomas D., ed. *SF: The Other Side of Realism: Essays on Fantasy and Science Fiction.* Bowling Green, OH: Bowling Green Popular Press, 1971.

————. *Science Fiction Criticism: An Annotated Checklist.* Kent, OH: Kent State University Press, 1972.

129

_____. *Voices for the Future: Essays on Major SF Writers.* Bowling Green, OH: Bowling Green Popular Press, 1976.

_____. *Many Futures, Many Worlds: Theme and Form in Science Fiction.* Kent, OH: Kent State University Press, 1977.

Clarke, I.F. *Voices Prophesying War (1763-1984).* London: Oxford University Press, 1966.

_____. *The Tale of the Future from the Beginning to the Present Day: An Annotated Bibliography.* London: Library Association, 1972.

Davenport, Basil, ed. *The Science Fiction Novel: Imagination and Social Criticism.* Chicago: Advent, 1959.

DeBolt, Joe, ed. *The Happening Worlds of John Brunner.* Port Washington, NY: Kennikat, 1975.

de Camp, L. Sprague. *Literary Swordsmen and Sorcerers: The Makers of Heroic Fantasy.* Sauk City, WI: Arkham, 1976.

_____, and Catherine Crook de Camp. *The Science Fiction Handbook.* Philadelphia: Owlswick, 1975.

Delany, Samuel R. *The Jewel-Hinged Jaw: Notes on the Language of Science Fiction.* Elizabethtown, NY: Dragon, 1977.

Gunn, James. *Alternate Worlds: The Illustrated History of Science Fiction.* Englewood Cliffs, NJ: Prentice-Hall, 1975.

Hillegas, Mark. *The Future as Nightmare: H.G. Wells and the Anti-Utopians.* Oxford University Press, 1967; rpt. Carbondale: Southern Illinois University Press, 1974.

Ketterer, David. *New Worlds for Old: The Apocalyptic Imagination, Science Fiction, and American Literature.* Bloomington: Indiana University Press; Garden City, NY: Anchor, 1974.

Knight, Damon. *In Search of Wonder: Essays on Modern Science Fiction.* Chicago: Advent, 1967.

_____. *The Futurians, The Story of the SF "Family" of the 30's That Produced Today's Top SF Writers and Editors.* New York: John Day, 1977.

Lewis, C.S. *Of Other Worlds: Essays and Stories.* New York: Harcourt Brace, 1966.

Moskowitz, Sam. *Explorers of the Infinite: Shapers of Science Fiction.* Cleveland: World, 1963; rpt. Westport, CT: Hyperion, 1974.

_____. *Seekers of Tomorrow: Masters of Modern Science Fiction.* Cleveland: World, 1967; rpt. Westport, CT: Hyperion, 1974.

130

_____. *Strange Horizons: The Spectrum of Science Fiction.* New York: Scribner, 1976.

Nicholls, Peter, ed. *Science Fiction at Large: A Collection of Essays About the Interface between SF and Reality.* New York: Harper & Row, 1976.

Panshin, Alexi. *Heinlein in Dimension.* Chicago: Advent, 1969.

Patrouch, Joseph E., Jr. *The Science Fiction of Isaac Asimov. Garden City, NY: Doubleday, 1974.*

Philmus, Robert W. *Into the Unknown: The Evolution of Science Fiction from Francis Godwin to* H.G. Wells. Berkeley: University of California Press, 1970.

Rabkin, Eric S. *The Fantastic in Literature.* Princeton, NJ: Princeton University Press, 1976.

Rose, Mark, ed. *Science Fiction: A Collection of Critical Essays.* Englewood Cliffs, NJ: Prentice-Hall, 1976.

Rottensteiner, Franz. *The Science Fiction Book.* New York: Seabury, 1975.

Scholes, Robert. *Structural Fabulation: An Essay on Fiction of the Future.* Notre Dame, IN: University of Notre Dame Press 1975.

_____, and Eric S. Rabkin. *Science Fiction: History, Science, Vision.* London: Oxford University Press, 1977.

Science Fiction Writers of America. *Writing and Selling Science Fiction.* Cincinnati, OH: Writer's Digest, 1976.

Todorov, Tzvetan. *The Fantastic: A Structural Approach to a Literary Genre.* Cleveland: Case Western Reserve University Press, 1973.

Warner, Harry, Jr. *All Our Yesterdays: An Informal History of Science Fiction Fandom in the Forties.* Chicago: Advent, 1969.

PERIODICALS
Extrapolation
Luna Monthly
Science Fiction Studies